D0574765

WHAT IS CONTEMPORARY ART?

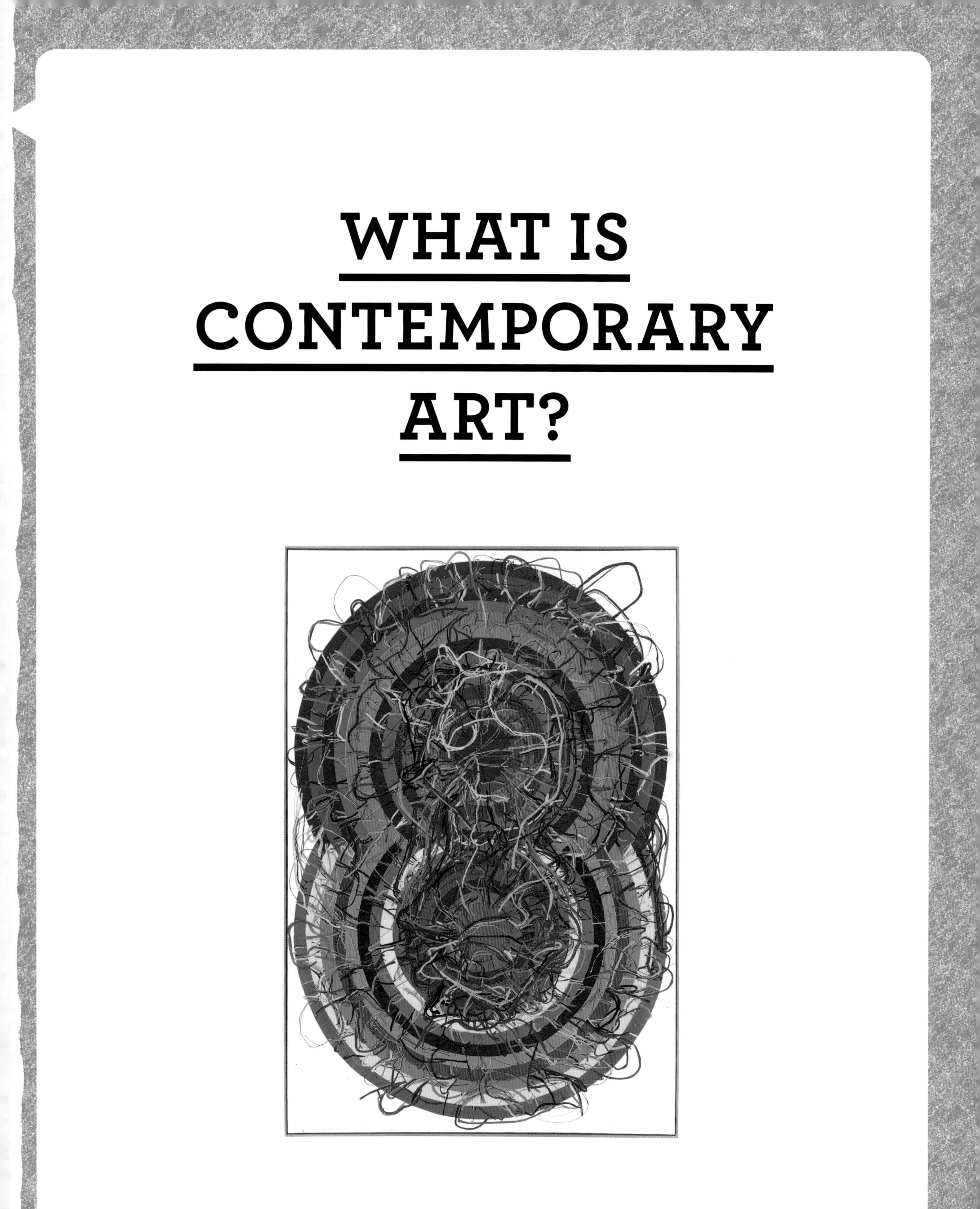

WHAT IS CONTEMPORARY ART?

A Guide for Kids

Jacky Klein and Suzy Klein

WITH 74 COLOR ILLUSTRATIONS

THE MUSEUM OF MODERN ART, NEW YORK

CONTENTS

INTRODUCTION 06

A SPLASH OF COLOR 08

LIGHT FANTASTIC 10

DRIPS, DOTS, AND WAVES 12

WHAT'S IN A NAME? 14

FACE TO FACE 16

GOING ROUND IN CIRCLES 18

BIZARRE BEASTS 20

ALL THAT GLITTERS 22

LINE UP 24

GETTING DRESSED 26

SEEING DOUBLE 28

ALL WHITE 30

FLYING HIGH 32

MAKING AND BREAKING 34

LIFE SIZE 36

38 SPARKLES AND CHOCOLATE

40 ORIGINALS AND COPIES

42 BALANCING ACT

44 READ ALL ABOUT IT

46 BLACK HOLES AND MOON ROCKS

48 OVER AND OVER

50 THE ARTIST'S BODY

52 PLAYING GAMES

54 BEDTIME

56 ARTISTS' BIOGRAPHIES

60 GLOSSARY

61 WHERE TO FIND OUT MORE

61 WHERE TO SEE MORE

63 INDEX

64 ABOUT THE AUTHORS

64 ACKNOWLEDGMENTS

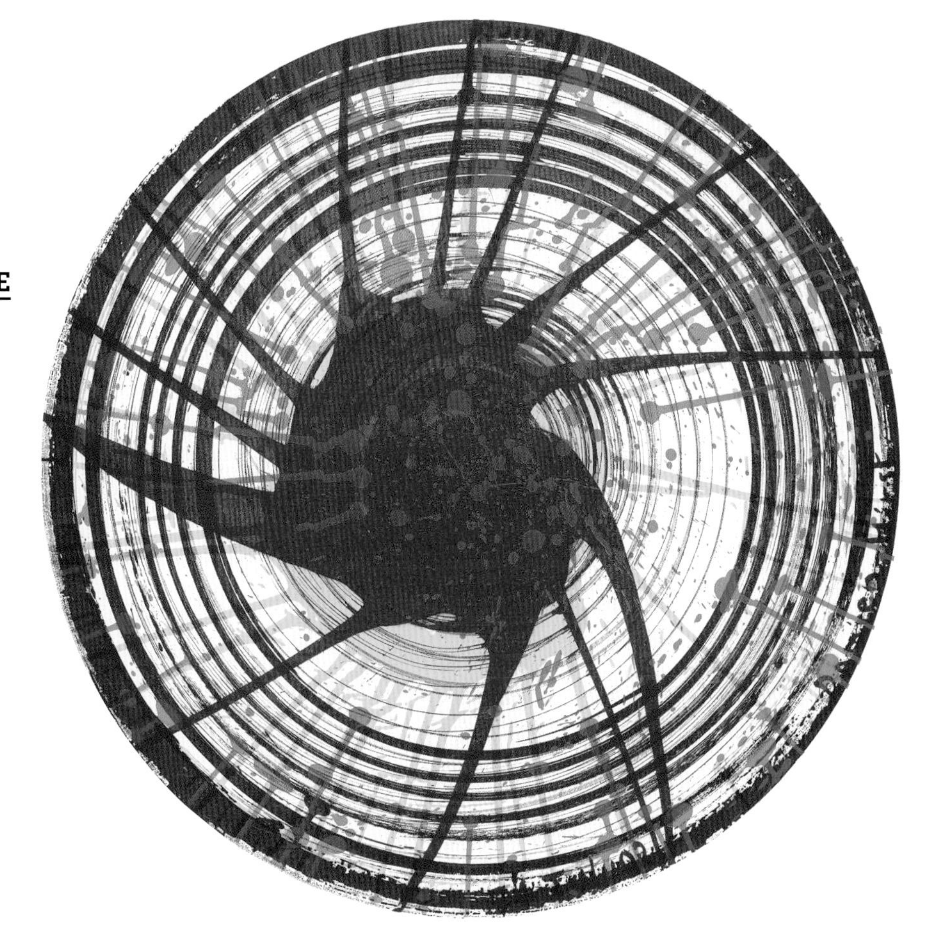

INTRODUCTION

WHAT DO YOU THINK CONTEMPORARY ART IS?
PAINTINGS AND DRAWINGS?
SCULPTURES AND PHOTOGRAPHS?

When you visit a museum of contemporary art, you will see all of these things—but you will also find much more. That's because artists are constantly inventing new ways to make art. They still use paint, ink, marble, and bronze, but since the 1960s they have also produced videos, put on performances, and made installations.

Artists today love to experiment and break away from tradition. They often use the most unexpected materials, like elephant dung, crushed cars, or chocolate. By transforming the things that we might think of as disposable and everyday, contemporary artists are always reinventing and re-imagining.

WHAT IS CONTEMPORARY ART? guides you through this exciting world.

Here, you will find artworks grouped together by theme, exploring the ideas and techniques shared by artists from across the globe. At the back of the book there are some helpful explanations of key art words—wherever you see the *asterisks,* just turn to the glossary. You will also find information on all of the artists in the book, and a list of useful websites and contemporary art museums showing where you can go next.

INSPIRING

This book includes artworks about games, outer space, and bizarre beasts. It explores the building blocks of art, such as shapes, lines, and colors, and it's full of art made from surprising materials such as electric light and empty eggshells. Take a look inside: which works do you find most inspiring?

Today, more than ever, art is about asking questions and setting your own rules. It's as much about ideas and feelings as how an artwork looks. Contemporary artists want us to open our eyes and see the world differently. We invite you to get involved—by looking, exploring, enjoying, and questioning.

WHAT IS CONTEMPORARY ART? Let's find out...

A SPLASH OF COLOR

Yves Klein, *Anthropometry: Princess Helena*, 1961

SOMETHING BLUE HAS SMEARED ITSELF ACROSS THIS PIECE OF PAPER. WHAT COULD IT HAVE BEEN?

The artist Yves Klein was obsessed with just one color: blue. He worked with a chemist to develop his own brand of paint, which he called International Klein Blue. It had a particularly bright and intense color. He applied the paint to his pictures using rollers, sponges, and even people! This work is part of a series in which Klein used naked female models as "living paintbrushes." The women were covered in blue paint and lay down on large sheets of paper, rolling around or dragging each other as directed by the artist. The body prints created by these *performances* made surprising shapes and patterns.

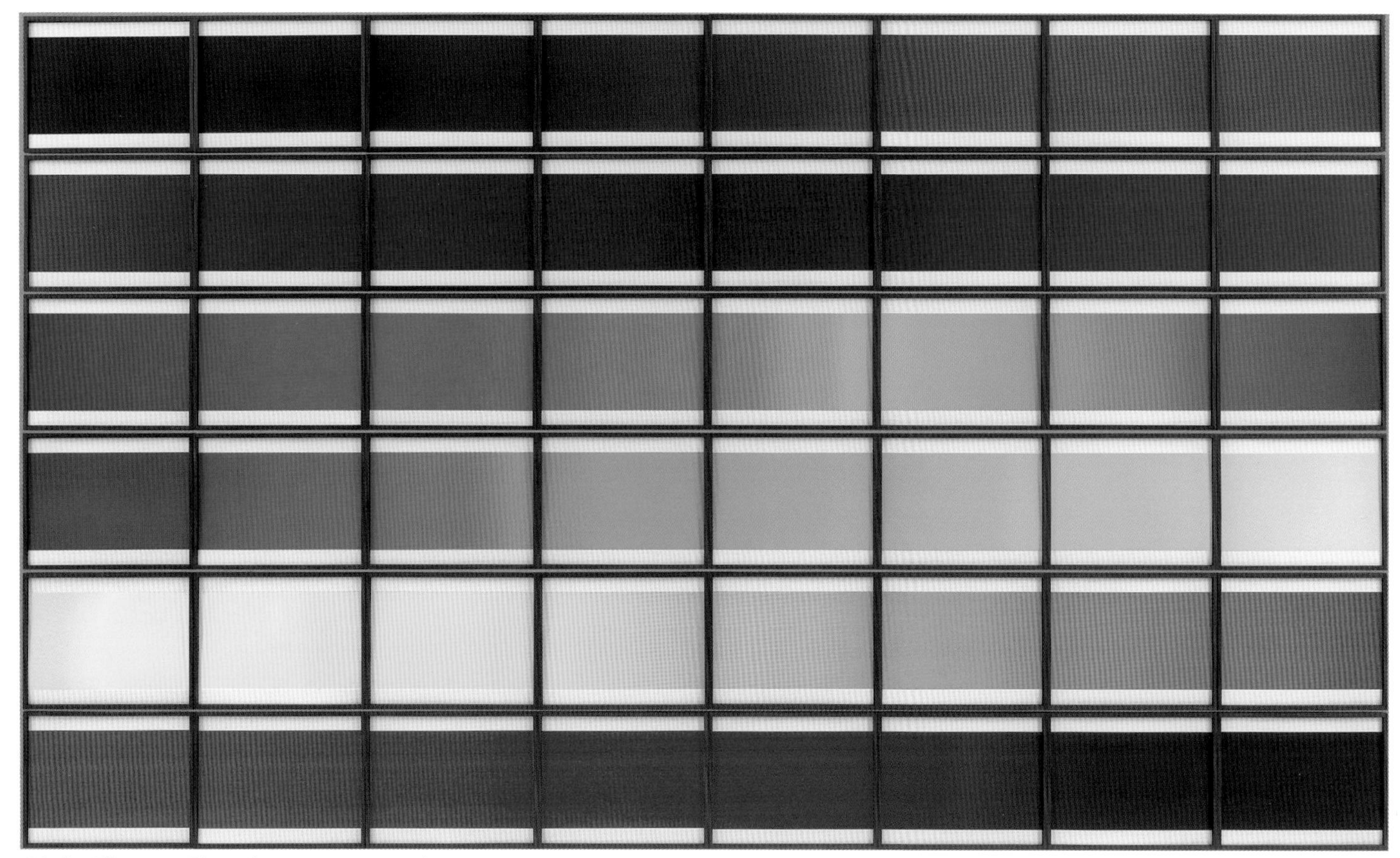

Olafur Eliasson, *The colour spectrum series*, 2005

A WORLD OF COLOR

Throughout history, colors have always had particular associations. Red can mean love or danger; blue often symbolizes loyalty, wisdom, or truth. Olive green is traditionally the color of peace, while dark green is associated with greed and jealousy. Imagine your favorite color: what does it make you think of, and how does it make you feel?

Olafur Eliasson likes to use the widest variety of colors he can find for his artworks. In the past he has created a giant orange indoor sun, made a real rainbow in a gallery, and dyed a river green. This block of *prints* shows us the complete range of colors the human eye can see, from deep violet at the top left corner to dark red at the bottom right. Eliasson wants us to think about how each one of us sees colors differently. Our understanding or perception of color depends on our memories and emotions, even our family background and which country we come from. When you look at the grid, which green seems most like an apple to you, and which is most like broccoli? Do your friends choose the same colors as you?

LIGHT FANTASTIC

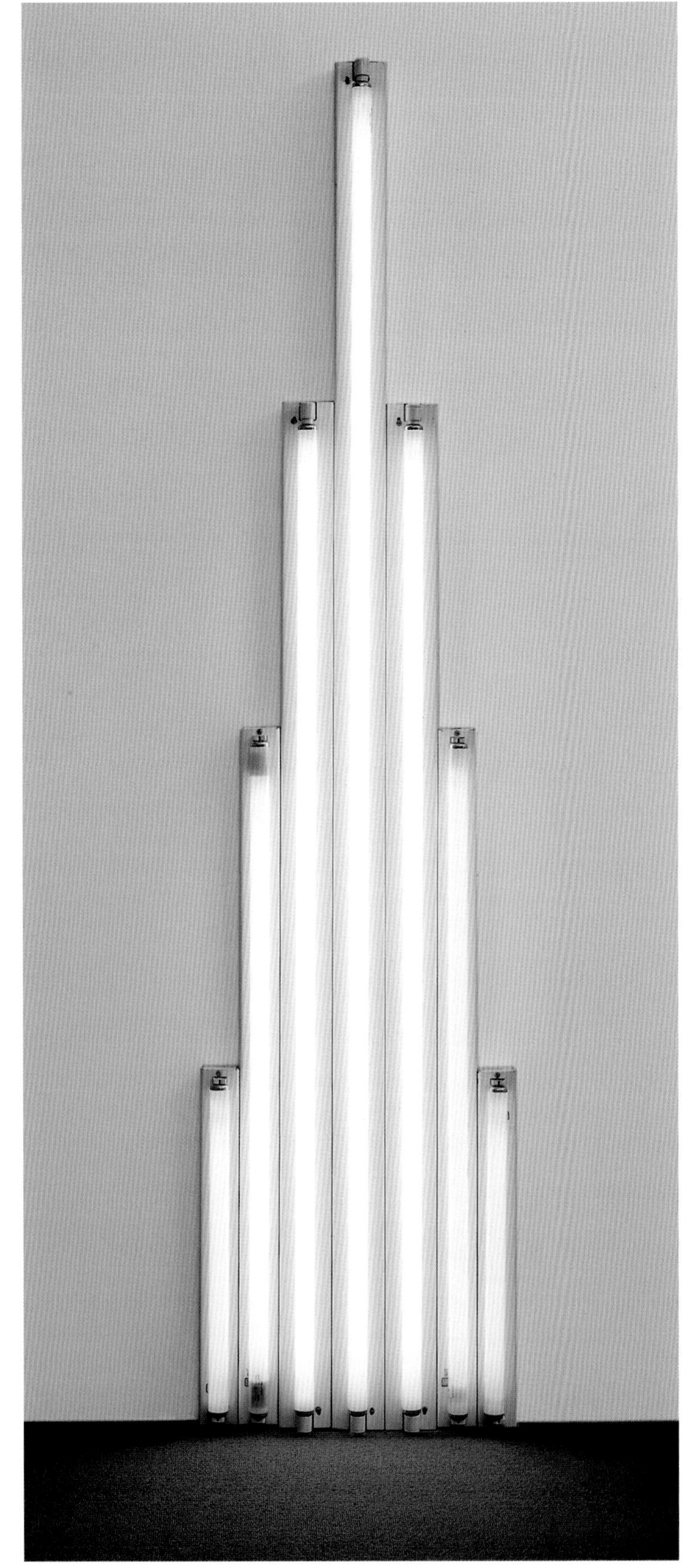
Dan Flavin, *"monument" 1 for V. Tatlin,* 1964

SOMETIMES SIMPLE, EVERYDAY MATERIALS CAN CREATE DAZZLING WORKS OF ART.

This light sculpture was made by the artist Dan Flavin using fluorescent tubes that he attached to the wall. Flavin liked to work with standard lightbulbs that he could buy in a regular hardware store. The bulbs offered him a new material for his art, and a fixed system of shapes and colors that he found he could adapt into countless different arrangements. This sculpture gives off a bright white light, but if you look closely, the wall around it also seems to shine. Can you spot the delicate halo all around the edge? What effect do you think this has on the artwork?

FIVE SHAPES, TEN COLORS

Dan Flavin used a very limited range of bulbs in his work, even though many more were available. He chose just five shapes (a circular bulb and four straight ones of varying lengths) and only ten colors (red, blue, green, pink, yellow, ultraviolet, and four different shades of white).

This work by Bruce Nauman is like a poem written in light. Nauman makes letters out of glass neon tubes, which can be bent into any shape he wants. Neon is bright and eye-catching, and is often used to advertise places such as beauty parlors or fast-food restaurants. But Nauman isn't trying to sell us a product. Instead, he uses flashing neon to create words that ask us to look deep inside ourselves. What do you desire, need, or hope for?

LIGHT ART

Artists have always been interested in light. For centuries, painters have depicted blazing sunshine, gloomy shadows, or light streaming through windows. The two artists here use real electric light to create their work. But what happens when the lights are switched off?

Bruce Nauman, *Human/Need/Desire*, 1983

Jackson Pollock, ***White Light***, 1954

DRIPS, DOTS, AND WAVES

LOOK AT THIS EXPLOSIVE PAINTING BY THE ARTIST JACKSON POLLOCK.

Pollock was known as an *Abstract Expressionist.* He liked to express his feelings through color and line rather than painting real or recognizable objects. Every part of this painting asks for your attention, all at once. Where do your eyes lead you?

DRIPS AND SPLATTERS

Jackson Pollock dripped and threw paint onto his canvases, moving the colors around with trowels and knives instead of brushes. His technique became so famous he was known as "Jack the Dripper!"

Roy Lichtenstein, *Girl with Ball*, 1961

This might look like a picture from a magazine but it is a carefully constructed painting, inspired by an advertisement for a holiday resort. Roy Lichtenstein often copied the simple style and *primary colors* of the comic books he had loved as a child. Here, he paints the girl's skin using small dots, making her appear as if she has been printed in a newspaper or comic strip.

Bridget Riley uses a different technique in her optical or *Op art* paintings. She creates visual illusions, tricking your eyes into seeing movement and vibration when your brain knows that you are only looking at lines on a flat surface. Concentrate on this painting for a few seconds: can you see the lines begin to dance and wave?

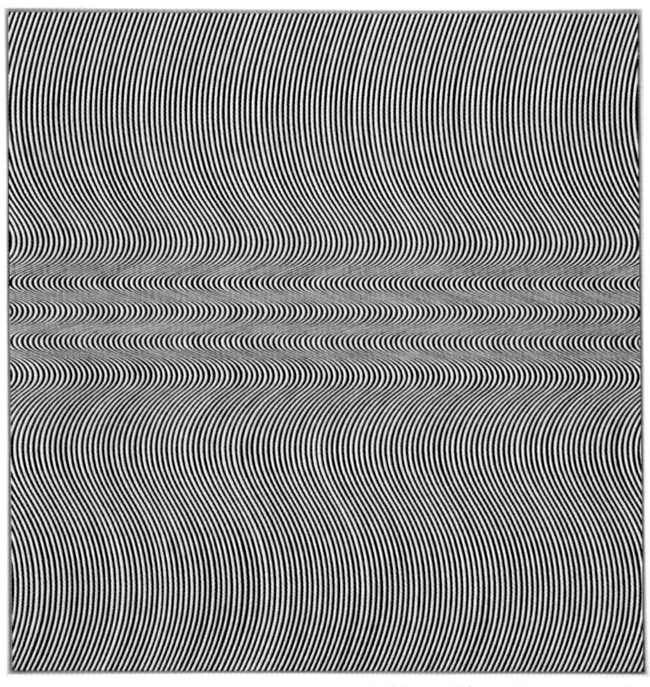

Bridget Riley, *Current*, 1964

WHAT'S IN A NAME?

THESE ARTWORKS HAVE ONE THING IN COMMON: NONE OF THEM HAS A TITLE. WHY DO YOU THINK THAT IS?

This painting made with white crayon on gray paint is by Cy Twombly. It's known as one of his "Blackboard Paintings" because the scrawled lines look like chalk on a blackboard. Twombly lived in Rome, Italy, and his scribbles are similar to the graffiti on the city's monuments and walls. But it is impossible to identify any words here. Twombly deliberately made his painting mysterious rather than clear or readable, so that we can find our own meanings in it.

HOW DID HE DO IT?

Twombly's painting is huge: the size of a small movie screen. He couldn't easily reach the top of the canvas, so he invented a clever technique: he sat on the shoulders of his *studio assistant,* Nicola del Roscio, who shuttled back and forth along the canvas. This allowed Twombly to continue his long, unbroken lines.

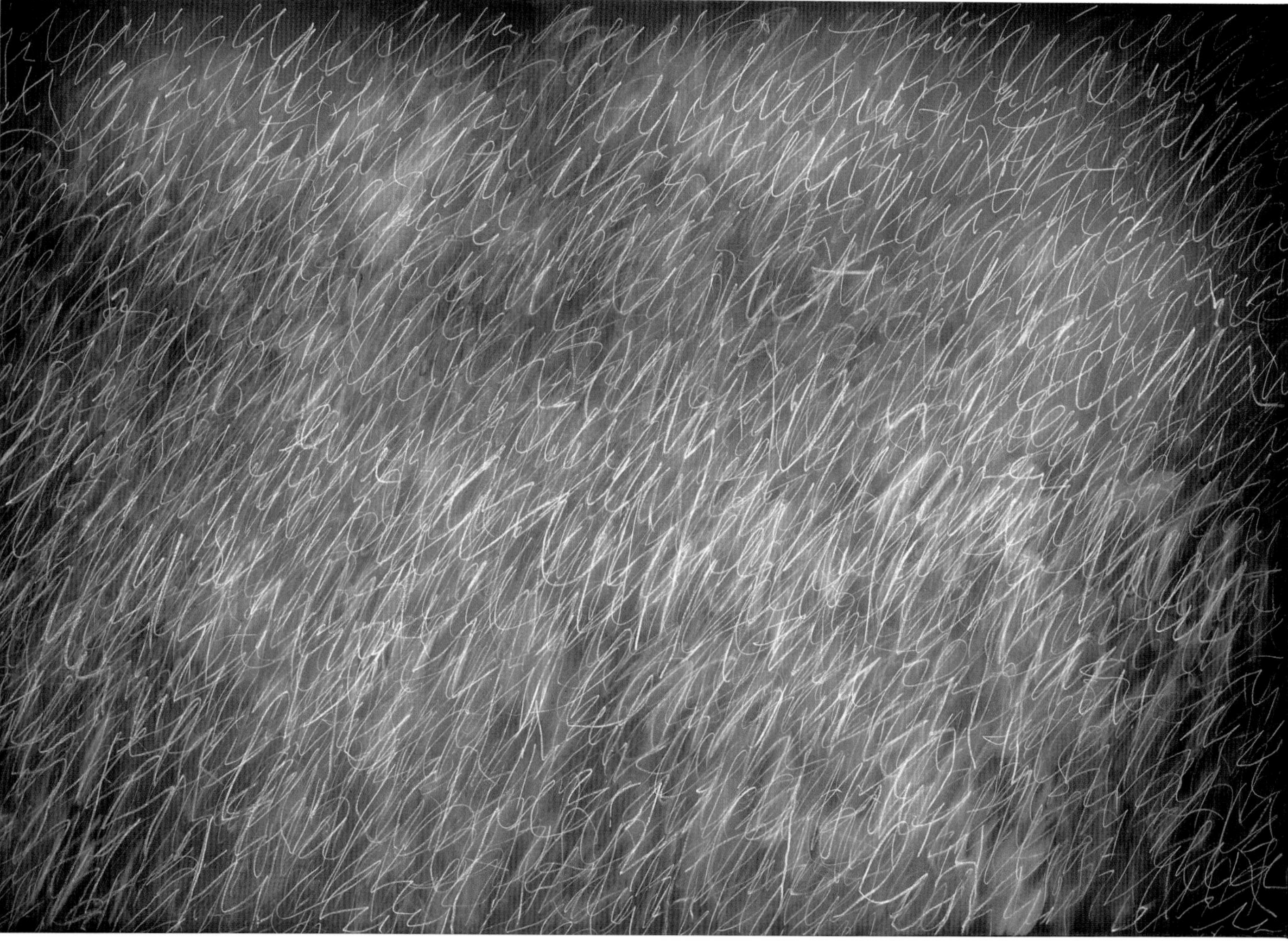

Cy Twombly, *Untitled*, 1970

"Random piling, loose stacking, hanging, give passing form to the material.... Chance is accepted...."

Robert Morris

What do these drooping parallel strips look like to you? Robert Morris's early sculptures were made of rigid materials, such as steel, but he switched to working with soft materials, such as felt, because he wanted to introduce movement and chance into his work. Here, the cut panels of felt hang from the gallery wall and sag in the middle. Gravity plays an important part in the shape of the artwork. Morris's soft sculptures could also be piled up or stacked on the floor, allowing the same piece to make different shapes. He didn't give titles to these sculptures because they can be moved and changed, so their meaning can change too.

Robert Morris, *Untitled*, 1969

Nam June Paik, *Untitled*, 1993

Nam June Paik was a composer and pioneer of *video art.* In this untitled sculpture, a piano without a pianist mechanically plays ragtime music. Two cameras record the piano's inner workings, relaying the images onto thirteen television screens. Two more monitors show the image of the composer John Cage, whose ideas strongly influenced Paik. This work was left untitled to allow its meaning to stay open-ended.

UNTITLED ART

Some artists choose not to name their artworks because they don't want to tell us exactly what to think. Instead, they invite us to come up with our own ideas. Ask your friends what names they would give these three works and see how many different answers you get.

FACE TO FACE

ARTISTS HAVE ALWAYS LIKED TO RECORD THEIR OWN FACES IN *SELF-PORTRAITS.* BUT THESE TWO AREN'T QUITE WHAT THEY SEEM...

This photograph by Gillian Wearing (opposite) is called *Self Portrait at 17 Years Old*. It appears to be an ordinary picture taken in a photo booth. But look very closely around her eyes and you'll notice something strange: the artist is wearing a mask. Gillian Wearing was forty years old when she made this artwork, re-creating a snapshot originally taken when she was seventeen. Disguising her face and neck behind a rubbery mask, Wearing carefully copied every detail of the earlier photo, including her hairstyle, clothes, and even the booth's orange curtain. Is this new self-portrait truthful or fictitious? Or is it somewhere in between?

HOW DID SHE DO IT?

Gillian Wearing worked with a team of hair, makeup, and special-effects artists to create her mask and wig. It was a long and expensive process, as the mask alone cost around $16,000. Wearing then took many pictures to capture the perfect image. As she says, "there is an art to making things look real."

Opposite: Gillian Wearing, *Self Portrait at 17 Years Old*, 2003

Chuck Close, *Self-Portrait*, 1997

At first glance, this looks like a pixelated photograph but in fact it's a painting based on a photograph. It was made using a diagonal grid filled with circles, ovals, and triangles. American artist Chuck Close is well known for his enormous paintings of faces. This self-portrait looks like the kind of digital image you might create in moments on a computer or cell phone, but Close's artworks take many months to complete as he meticulously paints them by hand.

GOING ROUND IN CIRCLES

CIRCLES CAN BE NATURAL OR MAN-MADE, ANCIENT OR MODERN, AND CAN SUGGEST STILLNESS OR MOVEMENT.

The stones in this circle come from Kilkenny in Ireland. They were picked up by the artist Richard Long after he took a walk there. Long loves nature and is famous for turning his walks into art. Sometimes he leaves an almost unnoticeable trace in the outdoors, such as some dusty footprints. At other times, he writes a poem, takes a photograph, or makes a sculpture for an art gallery. This circle has a timeless simplicity, like the still, ancient stone circles found all over England and Ireland.

UNIVERSAL SHAPES

Have you ever drawn a circle in the sand or dragged a stick across the forest floor? Richard Long also likes creating simple shapes in the landscape, from lines and crosses to circles and spirals. He has made circles while walking in many remote locations, from the Andes mountains in South America to the Sahara desert in Africa. Long uses the materials he finds on each walk—including slate, wood, or pine needles—to make natural shapes that echo the art of our prehistoric ancestors.

Richard Long, *Kilkenny Circle*, 1984

"I think circles have belonged in some way or other to all people at all times.... For me, that is part of their emotional power...."

Richard Long

Damien Hirst has made hundreds of paintings of colored spots and spinning disks. He is fascinated by objects that go round in circles—whether it's the earth rotating or an old-fashioned vinyl record playing on a turntable. For the *print* below, he put a metal plate onto a specially made "spin machine" in his studio. As the machine whizzed around, Hirst scratched into the plate with needles, screwdrivers, and other sharp tools. He then added colored inks into the scratched grooves and pressed the metal plate onto paper to make his explosive, whirling circle.

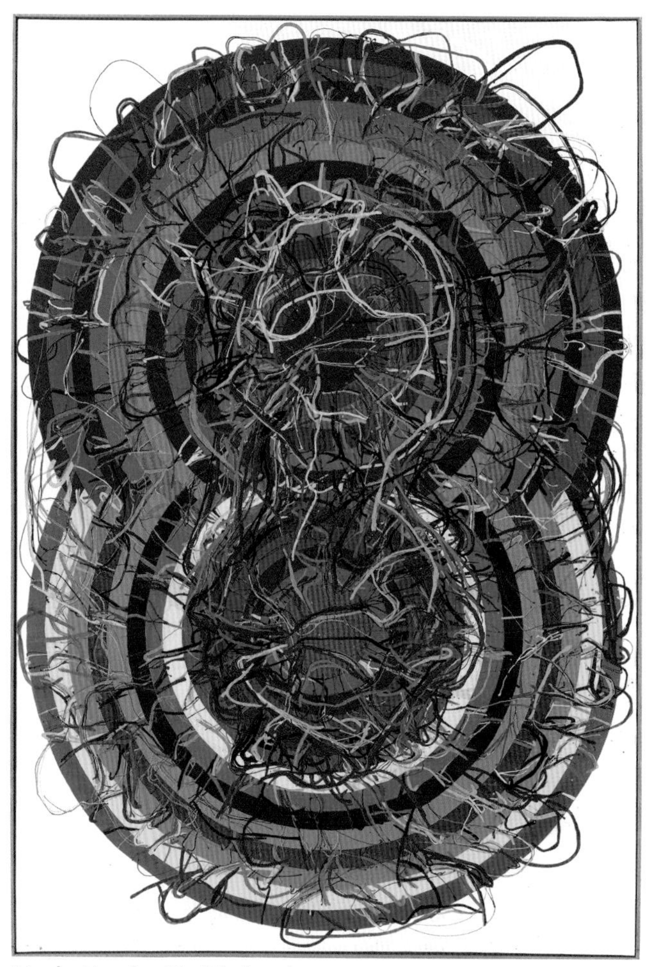

Atsuko Tanaka, *Untitled*, 1964

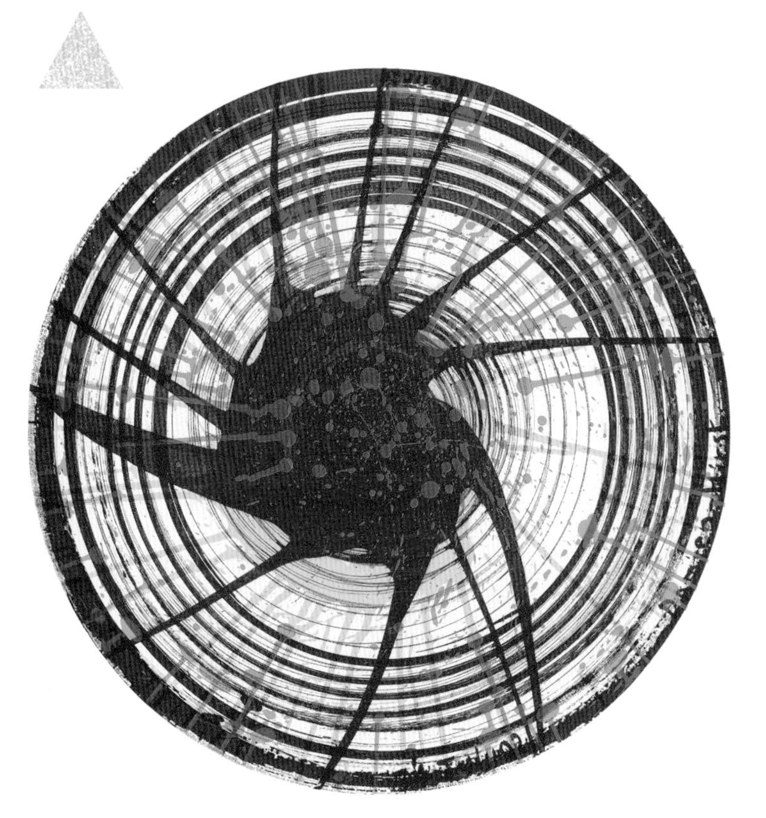

Damien Hirst, *Round* from *In a Spin, the Action of the World on Things*, Volume 1, 2002

What would inspire you to make a circular artwork? The inspiration for this painting by the Japanese artist Atsuko Tanaka came from an earlier sculpture she had made called *Electric Dress*. Tanaka was captivated by electricity and technology, and her dress was made from two hundred multicolored flashing lightbulbs. She spent much of the rest of her life responding to her wearable sculpture by producing artworks almost entirely from lines and circles. The trailing lines and circles-within-circles in this painting almost look like electrical wires and lightbulbs.

BIZARRE BEASTS

TAKE A LOOK AT THESE STRANGE CREATURES. WHAT DO YOU THINK THEY COULD BE?

Nicolas Lampert's hybrid beast is part animal, part machine. His chameleon on a tank is one of a series of fantasy photographs that also includes a stag fused with a train, and a praying mantis combined with a crane. Lampert pairs natural and mechanical forms to show the uncanny similarities between them. Here, both the chameleon and the tank are armor-plated, slow, and predatory.

MACHINE ANIMALS

Nicolas Lampert selects images from his own library of photocopies, then cuts and pastes them together by hand to make his machine–animal *collages.* He wants his images to look like they might be "a relic from the past, a lost scientific manual, or…a design for the future." Lampert loves animals and his art is a reaction to the destructive impact of both humans and machines on nature.

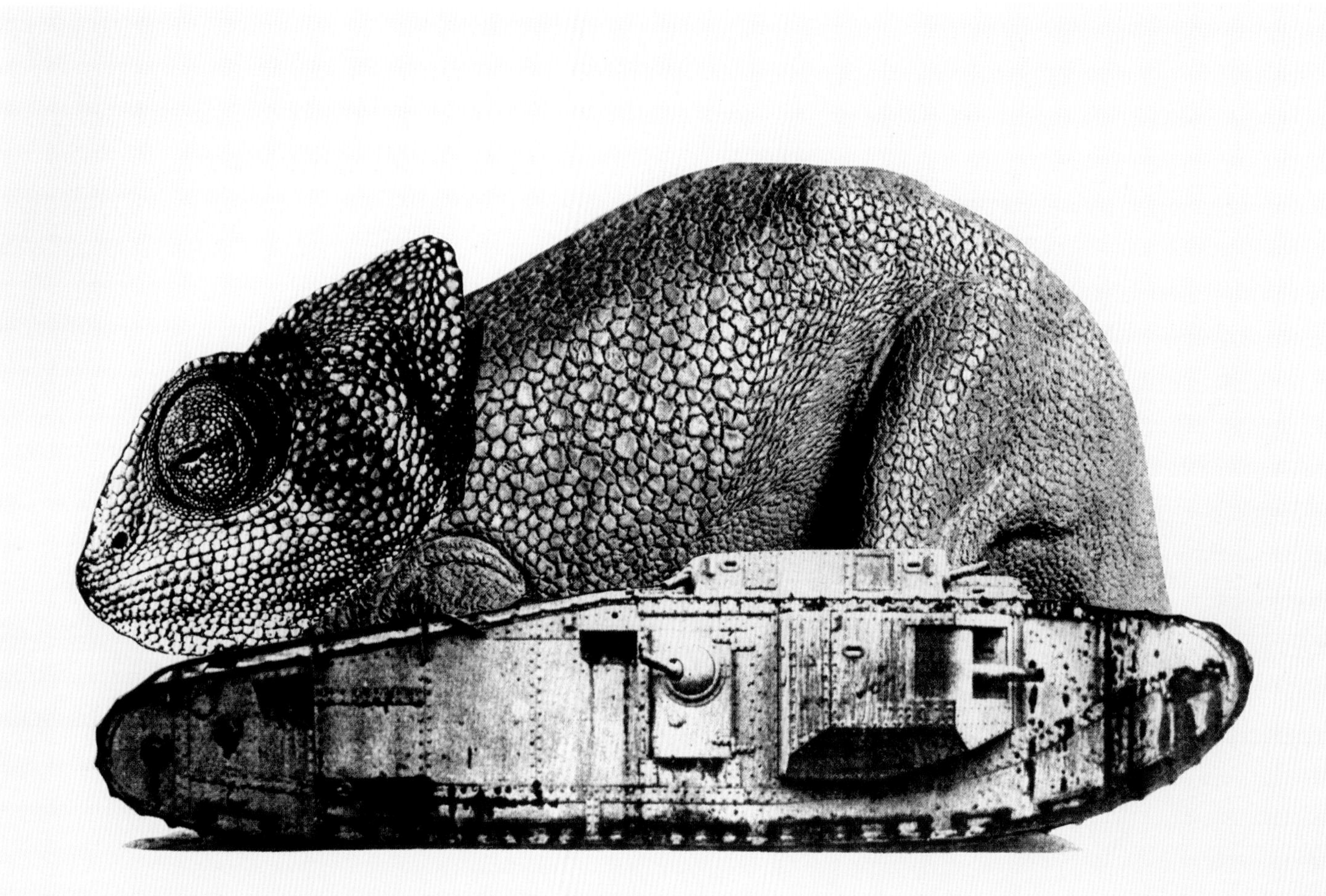

Nicolas Lampert, *Very Slow, Very Tired*, 2006

Have you ever seen one of these before? It's unlikely—because Joan Fontcuberta and Pere Formiguera have dreamed up another imaginary creature. They have photographically manipulated images to create animals that might be mistaken for specimens from a natural history museum. They call this beast *Alopex Stultus*, which translates as stupid wolf or fox, and they imagine it having the ability to camouflage itself as a shrub!

"The heart [of my work]... remains the questioning of photographic truth. Be careful, be critical, doubt.... This would be my advice."

Joan Fontcuberta

Joan Fontcuberta and Pere Formiguera, *Alopex Stultus*, 1985–88

ALL THAT GLITTERS

FROM ANCIENT TIMES TO OUR OWN, GOLD HAS BEEN ONE OF THE MOST ATTRACTIVE MATERIALS FOR ARTISTS.

This three-thousand-pound solid marble cube is covered in gold that has been beaten into thin sheets known as gold leaf. It was made by James Lee Byars, whose artworks were shaped by a quest for perfection. Byars had an interest in Eastern religion and philosophy, and *The Table of Perfect* is intended to be shown in the centre of an empty room, like an altarpiece or holy shrine.

THE ART OF GOLD

Where have you come across real gold? It's one of the rarest, most valuable materials on earth, usually reserved for jewelry and coins. It has also been used in religious art, from ancient Egyptian death masks to paintings of Christian saints and sculptures of Hindu gods. For artists today, it continues to symbolize perfection and divine beauty.

James Lee Byars, *The Table of Perfect*, 1989

Agnes Martin's painting *Friendship* is also covered in gold leaf. Martin is known for her delicate artworks featuring lines and grids, and here she has scored a geometric pattern into the surface of the gold. But her mathematical design is not intended to be rigid, and the shimmering painting is softened by the slight crookedness of her hand-cut lines. Martin wanted her artworks to reflect something personal, an inner emotional world. Her use of gold here suggests something precious and spiritual, like the very best friendships.

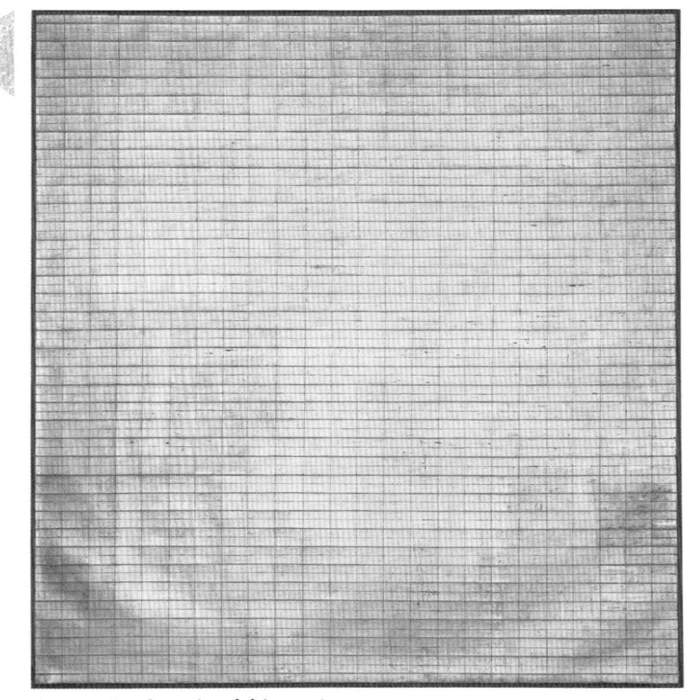

Agnes Martin, *Friendship*, 1963

Martín Azúa, *Basic House*, 1999

The Spanish designer Martín Azúa has made a very useful artwork that you can carry around in your pocket. His portable house was created from a light, thin material with gold on one side and silver on the other. The golden side protects you from the cold, while the silver shields you from high temperatures. Azúa's shelter is so ingenious that it can be inflated using sunlight or simply the warmth of your own body. Azúa has used gold because it is both beautiful and practical. Do you think his house is a piece of art, design, or architecture?

IN THE ARTIST'S OWN WORDS

Martín Azúa's gold-and-silver house was designed as a way to break free from material possessions and as an experiment in simple living. As he says, the house represents "A life on the move without material ties. Having everything without having scarcely anything."

LINE UP

DO YOU THINK THESE COLORFUL LINES ARE LEAPING UP OR FLOWING DOWN?

To make this painting, the artist Morris Louis leaned the canvas against a wall and poured down streams of color. He made sure the lines didn't smudge or blur into each other, but he was famously secretive about his painting technique and nobody knows quite how he did it. Louis left a lot of his canvas bare on purpose, so that the bright colors really jump out. It's the white space, as much as the lines, that make this painting so dramatic.

THE "UNFURLEDS"

Louis made more than one hundred line paintings like this. They were huge—so big that it was impossible for him to completely unfurl the canvases in his dining room, which doubled as his studio. At the time, there weren't many art galleries big enough for them either, so only two were seen in public during the artist's lifetime. Louis called these paintings the "Unfurleds."

Morris Louis, *Beta Lambda*, 1961

The Spanish artist Eduardo Chillida also played with the relationship between lines and the space around them. In this drawing, he used black ink, which he applied to paper with a brush to create a group of chunky lines. Chillida is best known for his massive sculptures made from iron, steel, wood, or granite, and the black lines here are similar to the thick interlocking shapes he used in his sculpture. Chillida loved to experiment with solid shapes and empty voids. As he said, "my whole work is a journey of discovery in space." The power of this drawing comes from the interplay between the "positive" space of the black lines and the "negative" space of the blank paper.

Eduardo Chillida, *Untitled*, 1966

Daniel Buren started making striped artworks in 1966. Almost all of his work features vertical lines of exactly the same width: three-and-a-half inches, or about as wide as an adult's hand. This painting on white-and-gray-striped cloth sits directly on the gallery floor. But Buren wants his distinctive lines to appear all over the place, not just in art galleries. He has planted striped rows of tulips, designed striped sails for boats, and even put his stripes on the outside of famous buildings, such as the Palais Royal in Paris. What's the most unusual thing you could imagine covering with stripes?

Daniel Buren, *White Acrylic Painting on White and Anthracite Gray Striped Fabric*, 1966

GETTING DRESSED

SOMEBODY HAS HUNG A SUIT ON THE WALL OF A GALLERY. WHY ISN'T IT AT HOME IN THE CLOSET?

Joseph Beuys based this artwork on one of his own suits—but it wasn't meant to be worn. Its arms and legs are too long, it doesn't have any buttons, and it's made of felt, which is too stiff and itchy to wear. Beuys repeatedly used certain materials, such as felt and fat, because they had special associations with his past. He often told a story about when he was a fighter pilot in the Second World War and his plane crashed in Russia. He was rescued by tribesmen who covered his injured body in felt and fat to protect and comfort him. So for Beuys, felt was not just a sculptural material but also one full of personal memories.

MULTIPLES

This is one of a hundred identical suits that Beuys made, in what is known as a *multiple.* Beuys made many multiples including photographs, films, and postcards. He wanted his artworks to be seen by as many people as possible and not just by the privileged few of the *art world.*

Joseph Beuys, *Felt Suit*, 1970

The artist Vito Acconci has taken another item of clothing out of the closet, this time from the underwear drawer. His gigantic bra can be placed in many different positions: on the floor, the wall, as a room divider, and even hanging from the ceiling. The canvas-lined bra cups light up and are so large that you can sit inside them, where you'll hear a recording of someone breathing and you might catch the sound of distant voices or music. Acconci's piece of *installation art* invites the viewer to climb in and get involved. If you sat inside his bra, how would it make you feel?

IN THE ARTIST'S OWN WORDS

"I want to make a situation where a passer-by says: 'It's a wall! No, it's a bra! No, it's a room-divider! No, it's the attack of the fifty-foot woman!'" Vito Acconci made his adjustable wall bra to surprise, confuse, and amuse us.

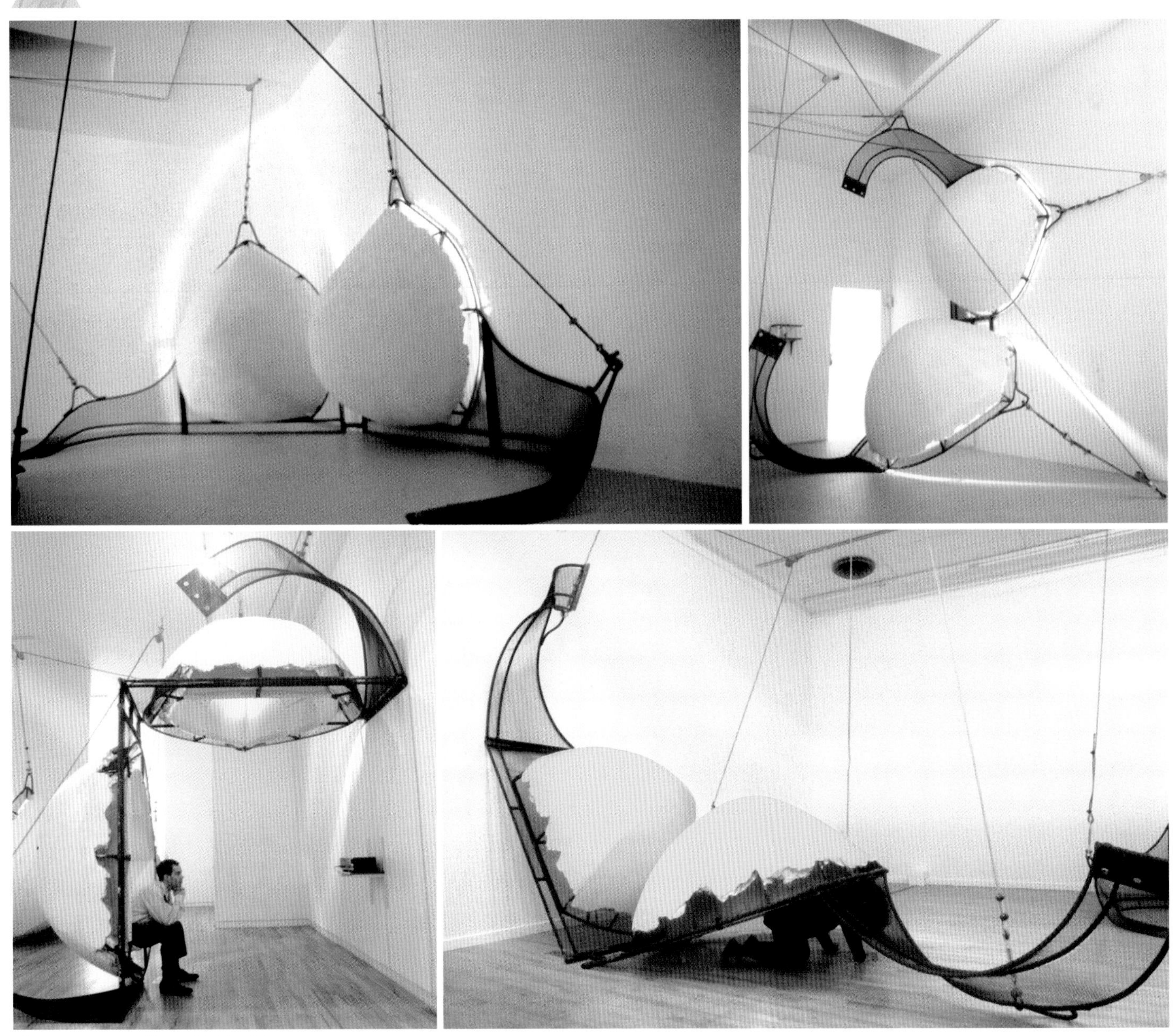

Vito Acconci, *Adjustable Wall Bra*, 1990–91

SEEING DOUBLE

CLAES OLDENBURG'S DOUBLE CHEESEBURGER SEEMS GOOD ENOUGH TO EAT—BUT LOOK TWICE!

These juicy burgers might appear to be real, but they're made of thick cloth covered in hard painted plaster. They were created by Claes Oldenburg, who loves to make soft things in hard materials and hard things in soft materials. Oldenburg is a *Pop artist* who is inspired by popular and commercial culture. Here, he celebrates America's favorite food with two burgers at nearly double their normal size. Does this doubling make them more or less appealing?

REMAKING THE EVERYDAY

Oldenburg has made lots of sculptures based on real objects, including lipsticks and tubes of toothpaste. He often experiments with size and materials, once even sticking a giant melting ice cream made of steel on top of a German shopping mall. Rather than copying everyday things exactly, he transforms and re-imagines them.

Claes Oldenburg, *Two Cheeseburgers, with Everything (Dual Hamburgers)*, 1962

Felix Gonzalez-Torres chose another everyday item to double up. He took two matching battery-operated clocks and started them at exactly the same time. No two batteries are identical, however, so one of the clocks will slow down first and fall out of time with the other. Gonzalez-Torres made this work when he found out that his close friend Ross was seriously ill. He knew that, like the clocks, he and Ross would eventually fall out of sync. His clocks make us think about the strong bonds that exist between people who love each other, and about how the seconds and minutes of all our lives pass by.

Felix Gonzalez-Torres, *"Untitled" (Perfect Lovers)*, 1991

Judith Joy Ross, *The Stewart Sisters, H.F. Grebey Junior High School, Hazleton, Pennsylvania*, 1992

This portrait might make you do a double-take: it's a photograph of identical twins. Judith Joy Ross took the picture as part of a project she carried out at her old school in Pennsylvania. Going back there reminded her of her own childhood, and made her think about how we all change as we grow up. These two sisters may look alike, but there are already many differences between them. How many can you spot?

"When I look at somebody I think about their past and what their future could be, as well as what I'm seeing right now."

Judith Joy Ross

ALL WHITE

WITH ALL THE COLORS OF THE RAINBOW TO CHOOSE FROM, WHY DO SOME ARTISTS PREFER TO STICK TO PLAIN WHITE?

Marcel Broodthaers took a table and a wall cabinet, painted them white, and piled them high with eggs. He was fascinated by *Surrealist art* in which unlikely images, objects, and materials were mixed together with surprising results. In this artwork, Broodthaers paired fragile white eggs with solid, antique-looking white furniture. The eggs he used are just empty shells that he described as "without content other than the air." He used white to suggest a similar kind of blankness, a lack of meaning. Try filling these eggshells with your own ideas: what story would the artwork tell?

Marcel Broodthaers, *White Cabinet and White Table*, 1965

ON DISPLAY

Broodthaers made lots of artworks about museums and how they exhibit their treasures. This cabinet and table are things you might find at home, but Broodthaers chose them because they are also a little like a museum display. The cabinet hangs on the wall as if it were a frame for a priceless painting, while the table sits on the floor like a pedestal or plinth for a sculpture.

"HOW TO PAINT"

Robert Ryman works almost entirely in white. He loves the subtleties of different paint textures on canvas or paper. By using white or off-white, he takes our focus away from the content of his pictures, encouraging us to focus instead on his techniques and methods. He says "there is never a question of what to paint, but only how to paint."

Piero Manzoni, *Achrome*, 1962

Robert Ryman made this white-on-white painting using twelve sheets of a heavy, cream-colored paper called Classico. He stuck these to the wall in a grid using masking tape, which he placed along the edges of each piece of paper. He then painted a white off-center square onto the joined-up sheets. Once the paint was dry, he peeled the tape off, leaving behind a ghostly trace of small, unpainted rectangles and lines.

Robert Ryman, *Classico 5*, 1968

Piero Manzoni chose white to make artworks that were as neutral as possible. He wanted to eliminate any outside ideas or references so that his art was about nothing but itself. He made white works using many different materials, including clay, bread rolls, cotton padding, and rabbit skin. This furry picture was created using white fiberglass wool that Manzoni shaped into hair-like tufts. It is one of a series of works called "Achrome," which was a made-up word. "Chrom" is the Ancient Greek word for color and "a" means without, so these works are not so much white as without color.

Andreas Gursky, *Bahrain I*, 2005

FLYING HIGH

THIS PHOTOGRAPH WAS TAKEN FROM A HELICOPTER, HIGH IN THE AIR. WHAT DO YOU THINK THAT SNAKING BLACK LINE ON THE GROUND COULD BE?

This large aerial image, taken by Andreas Gursky, shows the looping tracks of the Formula 1 racing circuit in the desert of Bahrain, in the Middle East. Gursky often takes pictures from high up because he likes to show us patterns and shapes that cannot be seen at ground level. He views the modern world as a place of advanced technology and vast scale where people are dwarfed by their environment. The cars on this track are tiny in relation to the sprawling asphalt landscape. Look very closely: can you find them?

IN THE ARTIST'S OWN WORDS

Gerhard Richter painted several bombers and jets before he made the *print* below. For him, airplanes in the sky are a reminder of his childhood feelings of "fear and fascination with war and with weapons...."

This *screenprint* was based on an image from a newspaper. Using a stencil and a fabric screen, Gerhard Richter applied pink and green ink to cardboard. He made the colors not quite line up so that the three airplanes look blurred as they speed by. Richter was interested in jets because as a child he lived through the Second World War in Germany and his birthplace, Dresden, was badly bombed.

Gerhard Richter, *Flugzeug II (Airplane II)*, 1966

MAKING AND BREAKING

SOMETIMES DESTRUCTIVE OR VIOLENT ACTIONS CAN RESULT IN NEW KINDS OF ART.

This painting by Niki de Saint Phalle is an *assemblage,* an artwork made by putting together or assembling lots of different things collected by the artist. Can you spot the metal seat, shoe, and toy gun? The work is from a series known as the "Shooting Paintings," in which Saint Phalle hid plastic bags filled with paint behind the wooden surface of the picture. She, her friends, or members of the public then shot at the paintings with a gun or rifle, bursting the bags and releasing streams of paint. Saint Phalle said she was aiming and firing at a society dominated by men. Her "Shooting Paintings" were acts of both creation and aggression.

BIRTH AND DEATH

Niki de Saint Phalle found an original way of bringing painting to life. By incorporating dramatic action into the making of her artworks, she created paintings that were also spectacular *performances.* As she said, "It was an amazing feeling shooting at a painting and watching it transform itself into a new being. It was not only EXCITING...but TRAGIC—as though we were witnessing a birth and a death at the same moment."

Niki de Saint Phalle, *Shooting Painting American Embassy*, 1961

Lucio Fontana has taken a sharp blade and with a single stroke sliced through this unpainted canvas. His action might seem like an attack on painting itself, but Fontana saw it as creative rather than destructive. His slashed painting was an attempt to transform a flat, *two-dimensional* surface into a *three-dimensional* object. Do you think this artwork is a painting, a sculpture—or both?

"Many people have thought that I was trying to destroy. But that is untrue. I have made and not destroyed."

Lucio Fontana

Lucio Fontana, *Spatial Concept: Expectations*, 1960

LIFE SIZE

THIS SCULPTURE SHOWS A MAN STANDING IN THE CORNER WITH HIS HANDS BEHIND HIS BACK. WHAT DO YOU THINK HE IS UP TO?

The artist Martin Kippenberger made a replica of himself, *cast* it in aluminum and dressed it in his own jeans, shirt, and shoes. His sculpture is called *Martin, Into the Corner, You Should Be Ashamed of Yourself*. Kippenberger made it after a journalist wrote something particularly nasty about his work. The artist's response was to create a life-size sculpture of himself facing the wall, pretending he had been scolded like a naughty child. Kippenberger was well-known for being a prankster who loved to poke fun at the *art world.* Who or what do you think he is trying to provoke with this artwork?

Martin Kippenberger, *Martin, Into the Corner, You Should Be Ashamed of Yourself*, 1992

In this sculpture, George Segal sat a life-size plaster figure on an old bus seat that he had found in a junkyard. Segal made dozens of life-size sculptures which he placed in real environments, using *found objects* such as a diner counter, street signs, and park benches. He was inspired to make this artwork after meeting a grumpy driver on the bus home one night.

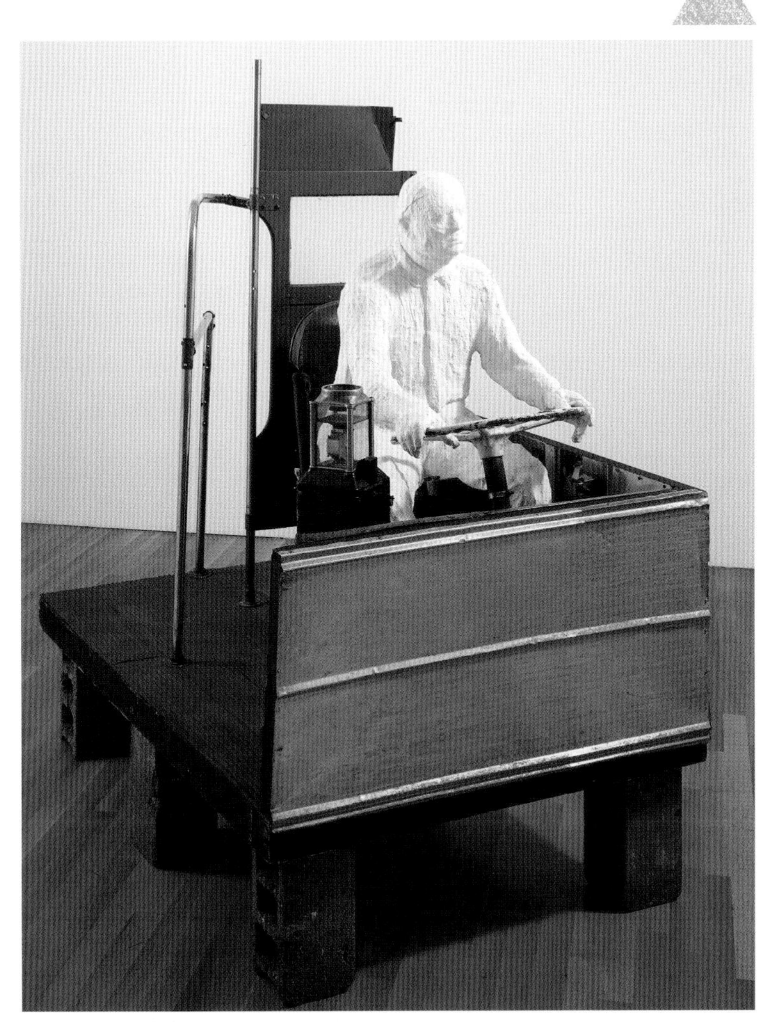

George Segal, *The Bus Driver*, 1962

HOW DID HE DO IT?

Segal's brother-in-law was the model for this work. He was wrapped head-to-toe in bandages soaked in plaster and had to sit very still. He breathed through his nose using two tiny airholes until the plaster dried hard. Segal then cut off the bandages, sticking them back together again to make a hollow shell in the shape of a person.

Michelangelo Pistoletto, *Man with Yellow Pants*, 1964

What's going on here? This man seems to be leaning against the wall of an art museum. In fact, he is a life-size image painted onto the surface of a mirror. Michelangelo Pistoletto's artwork often surprises people in the gallery when they catch sight of themselves reflected in the mirror and realize that the man is not real. It's an *interactive* work that changes as people move in and out of view. The gallery visitor is as much a part of the painting as the life-size man.

Chris Ofili, *Prince Amongst Thieves*, 1999

SPARKLES AND CHOCOLATE

WHAT'S THE MOST UNUSUAL THING YOU COULD USE TO MAKE A PAINTING OR SCULPTURE?

This painting of a man with an afro hairstyle (opposite) features lots of surprising materials, including sparkly glitter, map pins, and magazine cutouts of famous black people. Look carefully and you'll also notice three brown balls: one on the man's necklace and two on the floor. These are made of elephant dung, which the artist, Chris Ofili, got from a zoo. Dung has become his trademark, and makes his work instantly recognizable.

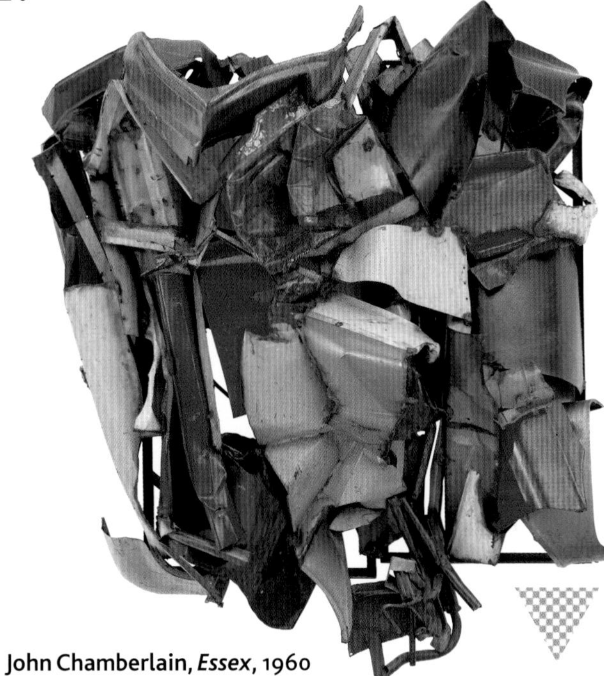

John Chamberlain, *Essex*, 1960

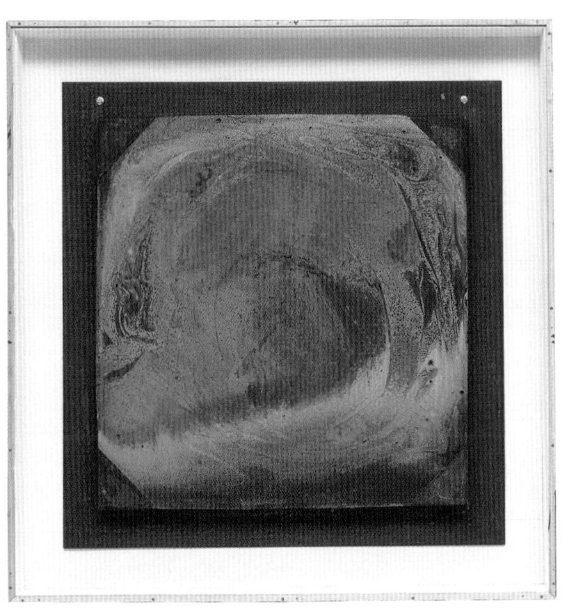

Dieter Roth, *Basel on the Rhine*, 1969

John Chamberlain used scrap metal to make his sculptures. He especially loved old cars, and he cut, crushed, and twisted their metal parts into colorful shapes. You might expect a used car to end up in a garbage dump, but Chamberlain shows us that secondhand materials can have new life, beauty, and meaning even after their original job is done.

Does this brown swirly picture look hard or soft? It's made from two very different materials: tough steel and gooey chocolate. The artist Dieter Roth often worked with food. He once made a sculpture with forty suitcases packed full of cheese. He liked making artworks that rotted and changed over time. This picture is slowly decomposing: the white blotches are the fats in the chocolate that have risen to the surface in the forty years since it was made. What do you think it might look like in another forty years' time?

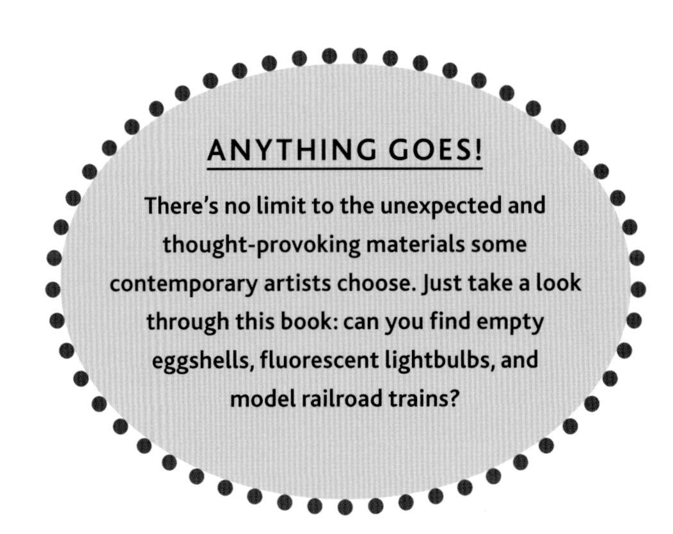

ANYTHING GOES!

There's no limit to the unexpected and thought-provoking materials some contemporary artists choose. Just take a look through this book: can you find empty eggshells, fluorescent lightbulbs, and model railroad trains?

ORIGINALS AND COPIES

SOMETIMES A REPLICA CAN MAKE US LOOK EVEN MORE CLOSELY AT THE ORIGINAL THAT INSPIRED IT.

The small painting on the wall at the far left was made by the artist Francis Alÿs. Alÿs lives in Mexico, where bright-colored, hand-painted advertisements are common, and he invited two local sign-painters to copy and enlarge his original. He encouraged them to change and improve his painting as they wished. What alterations have they made? And how does the presence of the two copies in Alÿs's *installation* change how we look at the original?

A GAME OF TELEPHONE

Francis Alÿs is a *conceptual artist* who is interested in ideas and concepts as much as in the final appearance of his artworks. This installation comes from a larger series called the "Sign Painting Project," which resulted in more than one hundred paintings by Alÿs and his team of sign-painters. Alÿs compared the series to an artistic game of "Telephone," where the original image changes in small ways each time it is repainted by another artist.

Francis Alÿs, *Untitled*, 1994

"[I wanted] to create a challenge for your eyes. I wanted your eyes to open wider."

Vija Celmins

Vija Celmins is also interested in imitation and replicas. In this work, called *To Fix the Image in Memory*, she displays eleven stones that she collected while on a walk in northern New Mexico. Alongside the original stones are identical copies of each that Celmins made in bronze. Can you match up all of the pairs? Celmins wanted her casts exactly to resemble the stones she had found, encouraging us to look closely and intensely. Which stones do you think are real here, and which artificial?

HOW DID SHE DO IT?

Celmins picks up many stones on her walks, but she keeps only those with the most interesting surfaces and patterns. She kept these stones in the trunk of her car for a long time, occasionally taking them out to admire them. Eventually, she decided to make copies of them, *casting* the stones in bronze. It then took her five years to paint them carefully by hand.

Vija Celmins, *To Fix the Image in Memory*, 1977–82

BALANCING ACT

CONTEMPORARY ARTISTS CAN MAKE US GASP WITH THEIR GRAVITY-DEFYING FEATS.

This steel sculpture by the American artist Barnett Newman is more than twenty-five feet high, or about as tall as a two-story building. It was made in the 1960s during a time of political unrest and race riots in the United States. Newman created his artwork using a pair of ancient Egyptian forms: a pyramid and an obelisk, turned upside-down and broken. Take a look at the tiny point where the two parts meet: the work seems to defy gravity. In fact, there is a steel pole hidden inside that keeps it upright. Why do you think Newman decided to shear off the top of the monument?

MONUMENTAL

Ancient obelisks were massive columns that stood outside temples as impressive reminders of death and the afterlife. Newman wanted his broken obelisk to suggest both sadness and joy. As he said, "I hope that I have transformed its tragic content into a glimpse of the sublime."

Barnett Newman, *Broken Obelisk*, 1963–69

Peter Fischli and David Weiss, *The Way Things Go*, 1987

When Peter Fischli and David Weiss worked together, amazing things happened. Their film *The Way Things Go* shows a series of finely balanced chain reactions in which everyday objects fall, rotate, and explode, propelling each other forward. The transfer of energy between balloons and cups, oil drums and mattresses makes for an inventive relay race. The film stills above come from a sequence in which a candle lights a fuse wire, releasing a tire which rolls across ramps and seesaws before toppling a ladder.

HOW DID THEY DO IT?

Fischli and Weiss experimented for a whole year to perfect their ingenious film. In the same way that other artists make sketches, they first shot a three-minute test film of key sequences to make sure they worked. The final thirty-minute film relied on a precise balance of chemical and physical reactions.

This sculpture was created by the artist Richard Serra using four large metal plates. What do you think is holding them up? Together they weigh a massive two-thousand pounds, or a ton, but they are freestanding and are not attached either to each other, or to the floor. Serra has been fascinated by industrial materials ever since he worked in a steel mill to pay his way through college. His propped-up sculpture might seem dangerous, as if the heavy lead slabs could topple over, but they are kept in perfect balance by the force of gravity.

Richard Serra, *One Ton Prop (House of Cards)*, 1969 (REFABRICATED 1986)

READ ALL ABOUT IT

THESE THREE ARTISTS USE LANGUAGE TO GIVE THEIR WORK ITS POWER AND MEANING. WHAT EFFECT DO THEIR WORDS HAVE ON YOU?

Korean artist Do Ho Suh often explores the idea of home and our feelings of homesickness when we're away. "Welcome" is a word we encounter at a boundary, when entering a new country, crossing a county line, or stepping over the threshold of a home. Suh lives between Seoul, New York, and London, and his doormat is an expression of how it feels to move between different places and cultures.

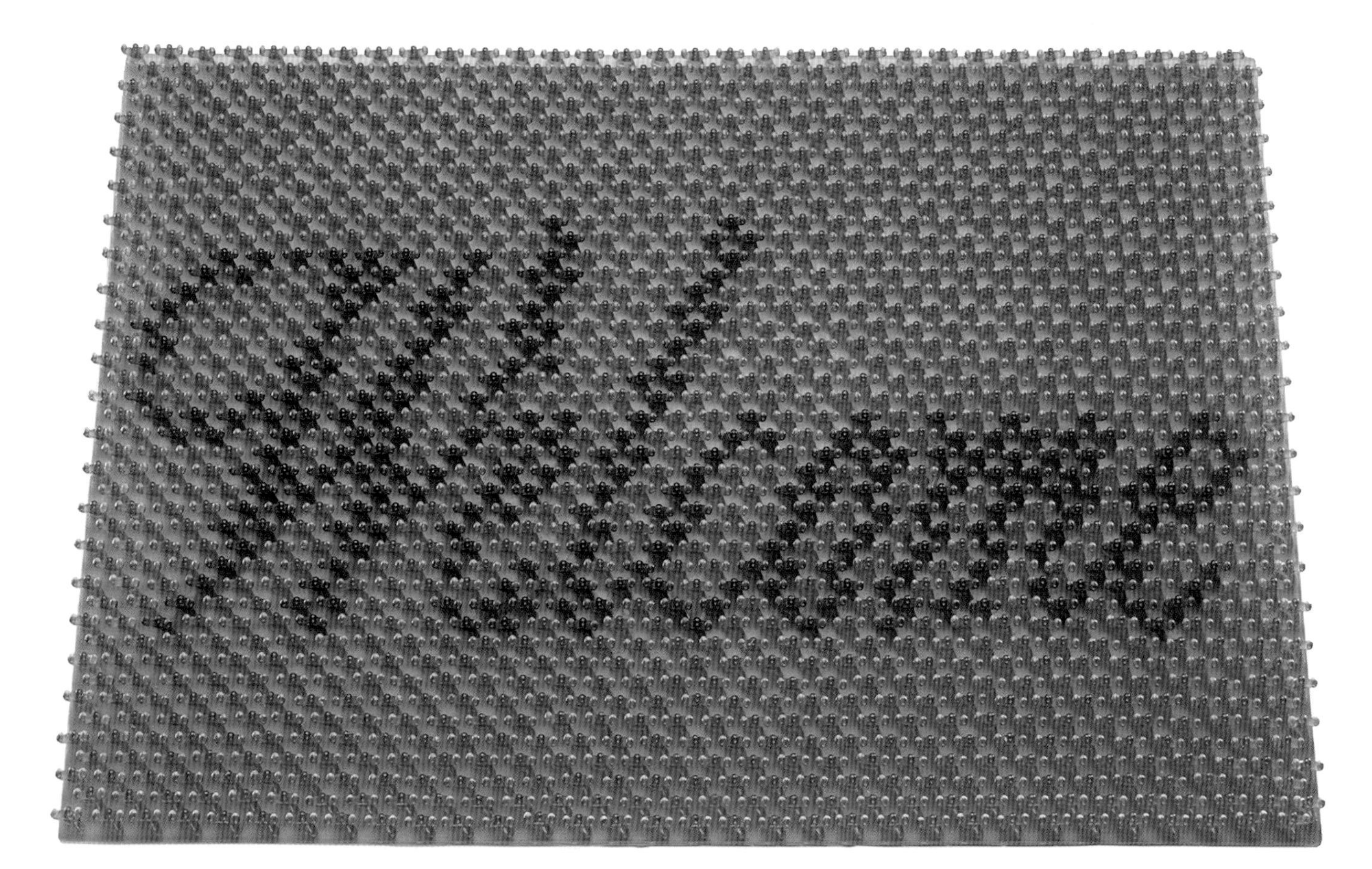

Do Ho Suh, *Doormat: Welcome* (and detail), 1998

ALL IN THE DETAIL

Suh's doormat is made up of hundreds of identical tiny rubber figures with their arms raised. Suh often uses miniatures like this in his work. He is fascinated by how we as individuals relate to each other and to the society we live in.

Ed Ruscha, *OOF*, 1962 (REWORKED 1963)

OOF! Ed Ruscha's large painting, as tall as a grown-up, spells out a noise of the kind you might see in a comic book fight. Many of Ruscha's paintings feature words on simple backgrounds. Just like advertisements, they immediately grab our attention. Ruscha studied *graphic design* and typesetting alongside art. His capital letters here are in bold type rather than scrawly handwriting, making them direct and forceful. But his word appears alone, more like a sign or logo than part of a story. What sounds and actions does the painting conjure up for you?

WORDPLAY

Over the last hundred years, words have become an ever-more important element in art. Artists love things that are a bit unclear, and words allow them to play with double meanings. By using language in their artworks, they can provoke and instruct us, make statements, and tell stories.

This warning sign by Antoni Muntadas offers a bold message about our relationship with art and the wider world: that to perceive or truly understand something, we must get involved. Muntadas is a *multimedia artist* who works with photography, *video,* *installation,* and *urban interventions.* This sticker comes from a long-term project of printed works written in different languages. The *series* is all about words, their translation, and their interpretation.

WARNING: PERCEPTION REQUIRES INVOLVEMENT

Antoni Muntadas, *On Translation: Warning*, 1999–PRESENT

Chris Burden, *Medusa's Head*, 1990

BLACK HOLES AND MOON ROCKS

TAKE A LOOK AT THIS GIANT METEOR-LIKE SCULPTURE BY CHRIS BURDEN.

Called *Medusa's Head*, this five-ton artwork is named after the mythical Greek creature Medusa who had snakes for hair and turned everyone who looked at her into stone. Instead of snakes, Chris Burden has used model railroad tracks and trains, crisscrossing a mass of steel, rock, and cement. What does his otherworldly sculpture make you think of?

SPACE

Some artists make works that look like they're from outer space, while others are interested in darkness and infinity. As Lee Bontecou says, "I like space that never stops.... Black is like that. Holes and boxes mean secrets and shelter."

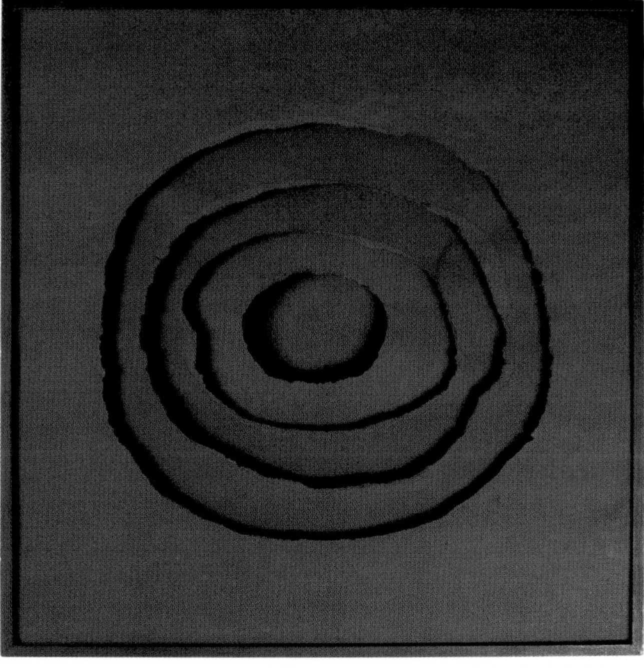

Anna Maria Maiolino, *Buraco Preto (Black Hole)* from the series "Os Buracos/Desenhos Objetos" (Holes/Drawing Objects), 1974

Anna Maria Maiolino has created a mysterious black hole by the simplest of means: layers of black paper that she has torn in circles and mounted on top of each other. Maiolino loves to cut and fold paper, and here she turns the flat, *two-dimensional* sheets into a *three-dimensional* sculpture, creating a sense of dark, infinite space.

Lee Bontecou is fascinated by outer space and many of her wall-mounted constructions feature voids and black holes. This one was made at the dawn of the space age in the 1960s, soon after the first satellite had orbited the earth. Bontecou used unusual materials in this sculpture, including rawhide and soot, as well as old canvas conveyor belts. These *found objects* came from the laundromat below her apartment.

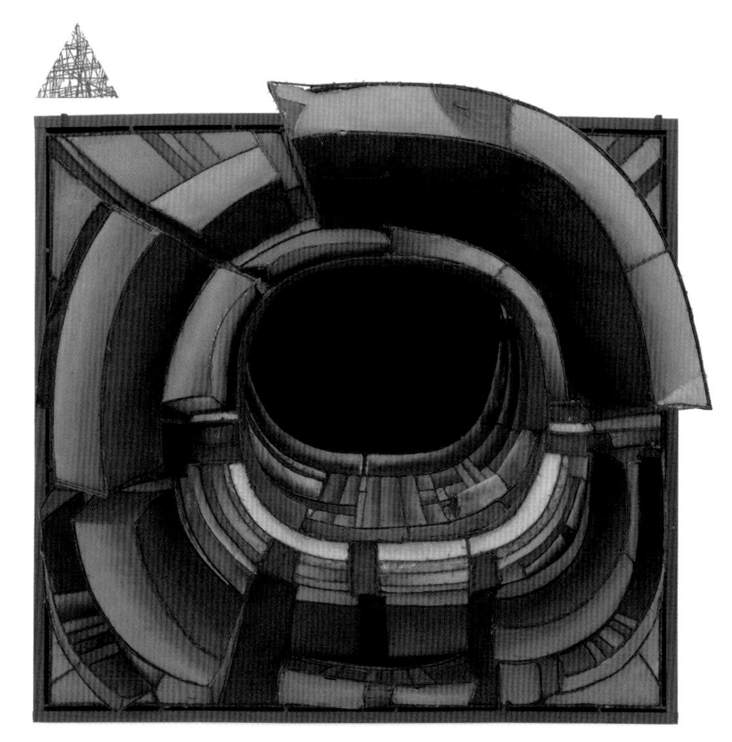

Lee Bontecou, *Untitled*, 1961

OVER AND OVER

Donald Judd, *Untitled (Stack)*, 1967

ARTISTS HAVE ALWAYS TRIED TO BE ORIGINAL, SO WHY DO THESE TWO LOVE TO REPEAT THEMSELVES?

Donald Judd's sculptures were based on simple forms that he used time and again. This stack of twelve identical green boxes hangs on the wall like a series of paintings but it also projects outward into the gallery. Each box is exactly nine inches high, and the artist gave instructions that the space between them also had to be nine inches. Judd was interested in how the placing or * installation * of a sculpture affects the way we feel about it. For him, repetition was a way of drawing our attention away from individual boxes and toward the experience of the artwork as a whole.

MINIMAL ART

Donald Judd was a *Minimalist* artist who liked basic, pared-down shapes. Most of his art was made using sequences of rectangles and cubes that either sat on the floor or ran up or across the wall. He wanted the individual parts of his sculptures to be identical, so he had them produced in industrial workshops rather than making them by hand.

REPEAT AND REWORK

When Andy Warhol found a subject that excited him, he came back to it again and again. He captured the soup can in countless paintings, prints, watercolors, and drawings. He focused on subjects that he loved, whether it was soup or Coca-Cola, dollar bills or movie stars. What are your favorite things and how would you make an artwork inspired by them?

Take a close look at these thirty-two paintings of Campbell's soup cans: can you spot the differences between them? At first glance they appear to be identical, but Andy Warhol made each one with a different label, showing all the varieties of Campbell's soup that were then available. Every can here is the same size and shape because Warhol wanted to highlight how similar and even monotonous they looked. His originality lay in his repetition of images from everyday life, and his transformation of cheap consumer goods into works of art.

"I used to drink [Campbell's soup]. I used to have the same lunch every day, for twenty years...the same thing over and over again."

Andy Warhol

Andy Warhol, *Campbell's Soup Cans*, 1962

THE ARTIST'S BODY

CONTEMPORARY ARTISTS OFTEN USE THEIR OWN BODIES AS THE INSPIRATION FOR THEIR ART.

What kind of body do you see here? John Coplans pointed his camera at his own knobby knees and wrinkled hands to show us a very honest portrait of his aging body. He started making black-and-white photographs after he turned sixty, to document himself in old age. His images encourage us to think about what makes a body beautiful or ugly.

TIMELESS

John Coplans only ever photographed himself, but he never showed his own face because he wanted his images to be anonymous and universal. Without clothes, his body could belong to any man from any time or place. As he said, "unclothed, it belongs to the past, present and future. It is classless, without country [or] language...."

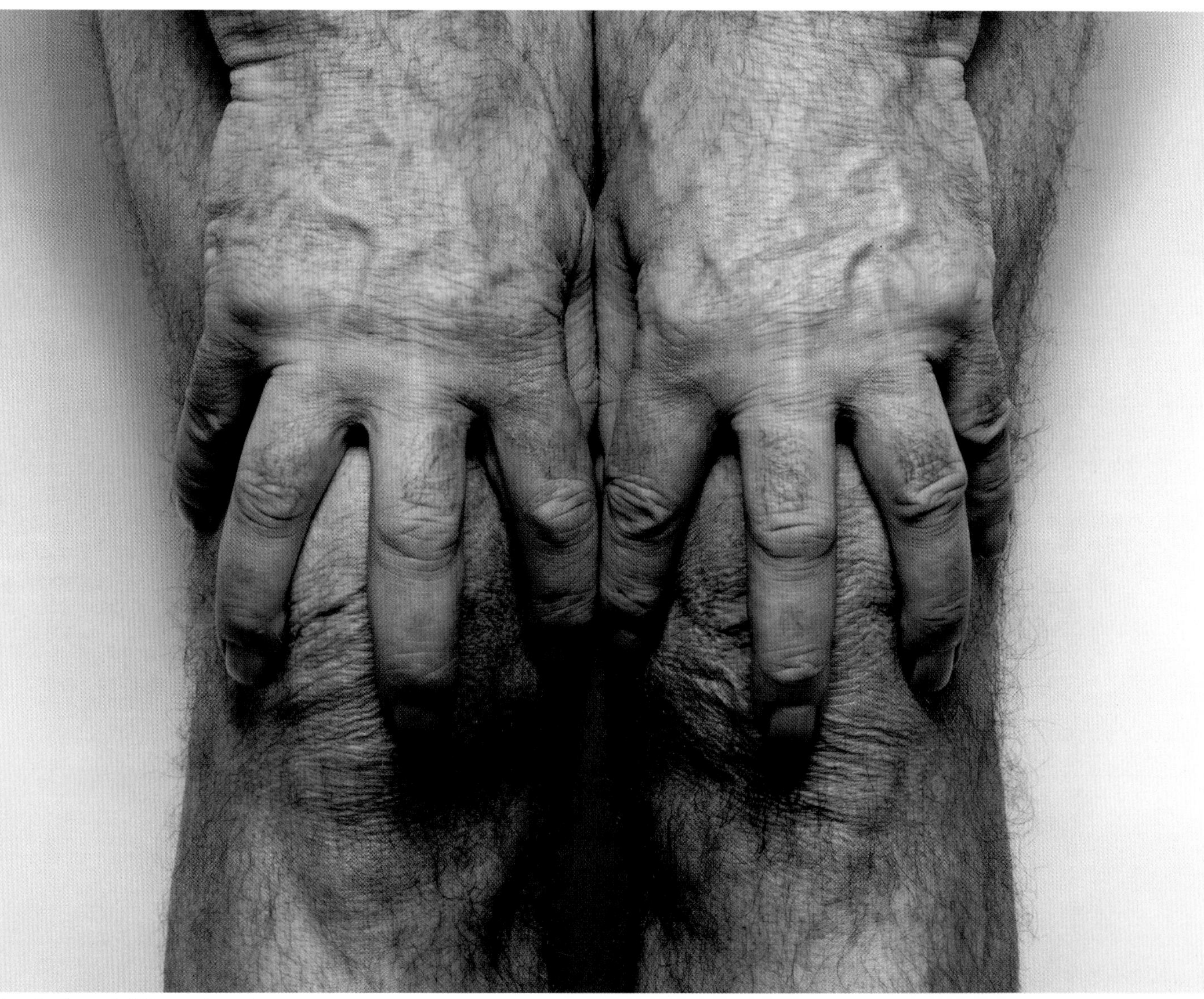

John Coplans, *Self Portrait*, 1985

Have you ever put your hand into paint, pressed it onto paper, and made a handprint? Janine Antoni used her eyelashes in the same way. She put on lots of mascara, brought her face up close to the paper and started blinking. Her beautiful *abstract* picture was made with the most delicate part of her body. What creative ways can you think of to use your body in an artwork?

THE ART OF PERFORMANCE

Antoni uses her body in all sorts of ways to make her art. She has created works by licking, weaving, and dancing, and once made a painting by dragging her hair, covered in dye, across the floor. For this drawing, Antoni blinked exactly 1,254 times on each half of the paper. All her actions produce artworks, but they are also a kind of *performance art.*

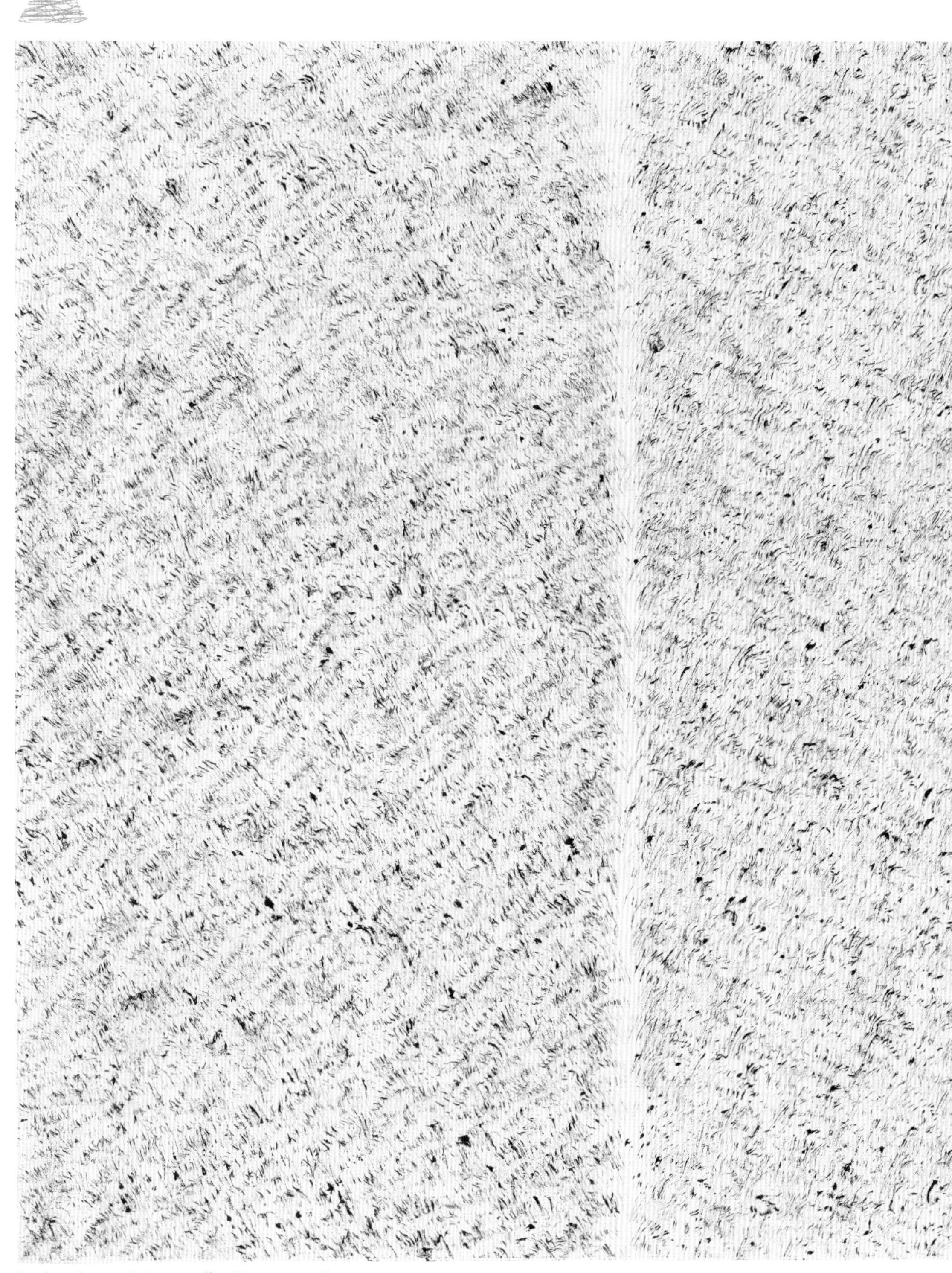

Janine Antoni, *Butterfly Kisses*, 1996–99

PLAYING GAMES

JEFF KOONS HAS SUSPENDED THREE BASKETBALLS IN A GLASS CASE HALF FILLED WITH WATER. WHAT'S HE PLAYING AT?

This is one of a series of tanks Jeff Koons made for an exhibition he called "Equilibrium," meaning balance. Exactly half of each ball is under water, and Koons worked with several scientists to achieve this effect. He has taken a popular, ordinary object—a basketball—and turned it into something extraordinary and worthy of our attention in a museum.

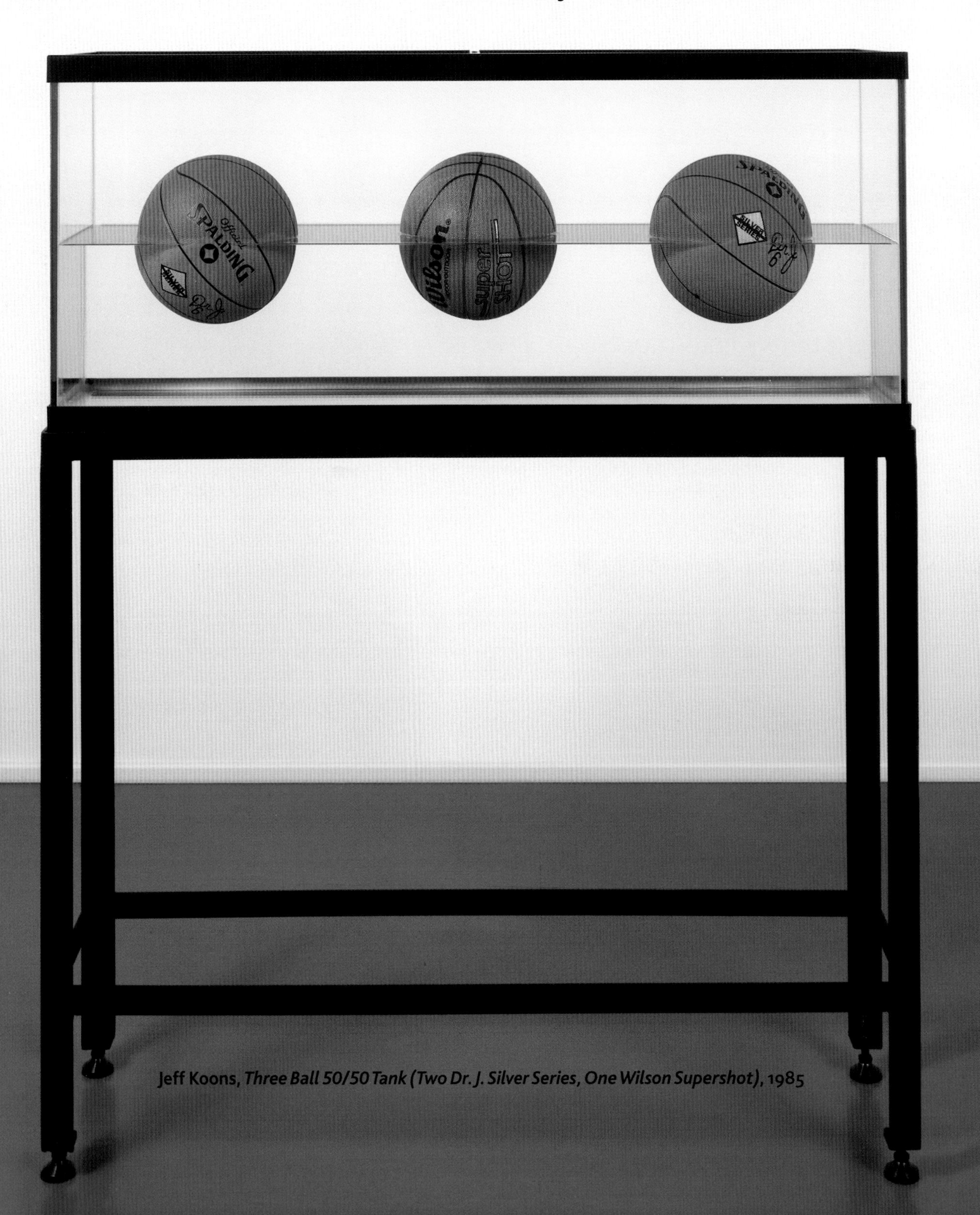

Jeff Koons, *Three Ball 50/50 Tank (Two Dr. J. Silver Series, One Wilson Supershot)*, 1985

Blinky Palermo, *Flipper,* 1970

This pair of *abstract* prints was created by the German artist Blinky Palermo. Called *Flipper*, it takes its name from the German word for pinball, which Palermo loved to play. The red, white, and blue geometric pattern copies the design on the pinball machine at his local café. In the left-hand panel, the blue lines have been removed. What effect does this have on the artwork as a whole?

RULE-BREAKING

What's your favorite game? The artists here were all inspired by a sport or a hobby. In each case they have either changed the game or broken its rules to create their artworks.

Gabriel Orozco has made an art out of re-imagining games, inventing a billiard table without pockets and a ping-pong game featuring a lily pond. Here, he has created his own version of chess. His board is four times the normal size and uses four colors instead of just black and white. Orozco has also left out all of the pieces except for the knights, or horses, so the usual rules of the game have disappeared. His chessboard is no longer a competitive battlefield but a landscape of the imagination.

Gabriel Orozco,
Horses Running Endlessly, 1995

BEDTIME

WE ALL LOVE TO CLIMB INTO A COMFY BED AT THE END OF THE DAY. WHY DOESN'T THIS ONE LOOK VERY INVITING?

Rachel Whiteread's bed is unmade: it's just a mattress. If you look closely, especially around the edges, you'll notice too that it's made of something hard—in this case, plaster. Whiteread made her mattress shortly after her father died, as a reminder that bed is not just a place of sleep but also sometimes of illness. Her sculpture transforms an everyday object from the home into a monument to sadness and loss.

NOOKS AND CRANNIES

Rachel Whiteread has made mattresses using many materials, including plaster, resin, and rubber. She has also *cast* other things from around the home, such as baths and dressing tables. Whiteread is fascinated both by the objects themselves and the spaces around them. By casting unusual places such as the undersides of chairs or the insides of wardrobes, she invites us to pay attention to the overlooked and unexplored. Take a look around your bedroom: how well do you know all of its nooks and crannies?

Rachel Whiteread, *Untitled (Mattress)*, 1991

Louise Bourgeois used her *autobiography,* or life story, in her art. Her work centered on emotions and obsessions, and often focused on her own family. Bourgeois's parents had a stormy relationship that deeply affected her, and she saw the bedroom as a place where family dramas were played out. The tiny figure here, dwarfed by a giant bed, might seem lonely or vulnerable. But this bedroom could also be a place of imagination and dreams. What thoughts and feelings does Bourgeois's bed inspire in you?

CHILDHOOD MAGIC

Louise Bourgeois made this *print* when she was in her eighties. Even then, the memories of her youth remained strong. As she said, "My childhood has never lost its magic, it has never lost its mystery, and it has never lost its drama. All my work… all my subjects, have found their inspiration in my childhood."

Louise Bourgeois, *Bed #1, state I*, 1997

ARTISTS' BIOGRAPHIES

★

VITO ACCONCI (American, born 1940)

Famous for: Sculpture, video, and performance art, especially an early performance piece in which he followed strangers through the streets of New York

Fascinating fact: Acconci's father made bathrobes for a living.

★

FRANCIS ALŸS (Belgian, born 1959)

Famous for: Conceptual and performance art, which often revolves around walking

Fascinating fact: Alÿs once got five hundred volunteers to move an entire sand dune by just a few inches, in the desert outside Lima, Peru.

★

JANINE ANTONI (Bahamian, born 1964)

Famous for: Performances that involve her own body, including sculpting portraits of herself from chocolate and soap

Fascinating fact: Antoni spent her childhood in Freeport in the Bahamas where she loved to make sandcastles on the beach.

★

MARTÍN AZÚA (Spanish, born 1965)

Famous for: Ingenious environmental designs

Fascinating fact: Azúa designed the medals for the 2003 World Swimming Championships, including a transparent, bubble-filled swimming medal.

★

JOSEPH BEUYS (German, 1921–86)

Famous for: Installations using fat and felt

Fascinating fact: Beuys almost always wore the same outfit: jeans, a felt hat, and a fishing vest.

★

LEE BONTECOU (American, born 1931)

Famous for: Wall-mounted sculptures made from welded steel frames and found objects

Fascinating fact: Bontecou's father and uncle invented the world's first aluminum canoe.

★

LOUISE BOURGEOIS (American, born France, 1911–2010)

Famous for: Sculptures and installations, especially her giant spider sculptures

Fascinating fact: Bourgeois loved cooking, and one of her favorite foods was oxtail stew.

★

MARCEL BROODTHAERS (Belgian, 1924–76)

Famous for: Artworks made using eggs and mussel shells

Fascinating fact: Broodthaers once interviewed a cat about its views on contemporary art.

★

CHRIS BURDEN (American, 1946–2015)

Famous for: Performance art, especially his early work that placed him in extreme physical danger

Fascinating fact: Burden created a performance piece while in college which involved him spending five days and nights inside a gym locker.

★

DANIEL BUREN (French, born 1938)

Famous for: Striped artworks

Fascinating fact: Buren has designed striped scarves for the French fashion house Hermès.

★

JAMES LEE BYARS (American, 1932–97)

Famous for: Mysterious performances, installations, and objects made from gold, glass, and stone

Fascinating fact: Byars often dressed in a gold suit and top hat.

★

VIJA CELMINS (American, born Latvia 1938)

Famous for: Detailed paintings and drawings of the night sky, the sea, and spiders' webs

Fascinating fact: When Celmins was young, her mother drew a picture of a pansy for her. Today, Celmins surrounds herself with the flowers to remind her of her mother.

★

JOHN CHAMBERLAIN (American, 1927–2011)

Famous for: Sculptures made from crushed cars

Fascinating fact: Chamberlain trained as a hairdresser and makeup artist before becoming a sculptor.

★

EDUARDO CHILLIDA (Spanish, 1924–2002)

Famous for: Large abstract sculptures made from steel or iron

Fascinating fact: As a young man, Chillida was the goalkeeper for the Spanish soccer team Real Sociedad, but had to retire because of a knee injury.

★

CHUCK CLOSE (American, born 1940)

Famous for: Large-scale portraits based on photographs

Fascinating fact: Close has a condition known as "face blindness," or prosopagnosia, where he finds it impossible to recognize people's faces.

★

JOHN COPLANS (British, 1920–2003)

Famous for: Black-and-white photographs of his own naked body

Fascinating fact: Coplans was a fighter pilot during the Second World War.

★

OLAFUR ELIASSON (Danish, born 1967)

Famous for: Artworks that re-create natural phenomena such as rainbows, ice, steam, and waterfalls

Fascinating fact: As a teenager, Eliasson was in a breakdancing crew that won the Scandinavian championships two years in a row.

PETER FISCHLI AND DAVID WEISS (Swiss, born 1952 and Swiss, 1946–2012)

Famous for: Adapting everyday objects to create witty artworks; known especially for their film *The Way Things Go*

Fascinating fact: The artists' first collaboration was a series of photographs called *Wurstserie (Sausage Series)*, featuring small scenes made with various kinds of sausages and meat.

DAN FLAVIN (American, 1933–96)

Famous for: Fluorescent light sculptures and installations

Fascinating fact: As a young man, Flavin was a guard and elevator operator at The Museum of Modern Art, New York.

LUCIO FONTANA (Italian, 1899–1968)

Famous for: Slashed or punctured canvases

Fascinating fact: Fontana would often spend days or even weeks looking at a painting before deciding where to make a cut in its surface.

JOAN FONTCUBERTA (Spanish, born 1955)

Famous for: Photographs that question the nature of truth and illusion, especially his images of fictitious hybrid animals

Fascinating fact: Fontcuberta has no formal training as an artist and started his career in advertising.

PERE FORMIGUERA (Spanish, 1952–2013)

Famous for: Photographs of his family and friends

Fascinating fact: One of Formiguera's projects involved taking photographs of more than thirty people once a month for ten years, to see how they changed as they grew older.

FELIX GONZALEZ-TORRES (American, born Cuba, 1957–96)

Famous for: Sculptures made from piles of candy

Fascinating fact: Gonzalez-Torres's father bought him his first set of watercolors when he was six years old.

ANDREAS GURSKY (German, born 1955)

Famous for: Large-scale, highly detailed photographs of supermarkets, stock exchanges, and apartment buildings

Fascinating fact: Gursky's parents were both professional photographers and taught him the basics of photography when he was a young boy.

DAMIEN HIRST (British, born 1965)

Famous for: Sculptures featuring animals in glass tanks suspended in formaldehyde, especially his pickled tiger shark

Fascinating fact: Hirst is a compulsive collector—alongside a huge number of contemporary artworks, he has also bought totem poles, skulls, a cow with six legs, and hundreds of fake Picasso paintings.

DONALD JUDD (American, 1928–94)

Famous for: Minimalist sculptures in metal, plywood, concrete, and Plexiglas, often in the shape of cubes or rectangles

Fascinating fact: Judd was obsessed by cacti and every time he moved apartment his desert plants came with him.

MARTIN KIPPENBERGER (German, 1953–97)

Famous for: A rebellious attitude and provocative artworks, particularly his self-portraits

Fascinating fact: Kippenberger's favorite food was noodles and he included them in lots of his paintings and drawings.

YVES KLEIN (French, 1928–62)

Famous for: Paintings made with his trademark blue paint called International Klein Blue

Fascinating fact: Klein had a blackbelt in judo and wrote a book about the martial art. After spending two years in Japan, he even set up his own judo club in Paris.

JEFF KOONS (American, born 1955)

Famous for: Highly polished steel sculptures of inflatable rabbits and balloon dogs

Fascinating fact: Koons worked as a banker on Wall Street while he was establishing himself as an artist.

NICOLAS LAMPERT (American, born 1969)

Famous for: Collages that combine animals with machines

Fascinating fact: Lampert has made a series of artworks called "Meatscapes," featuring enormous pieces of meat placed in a variety of locations, from the pyramids in Egypt to the American Wild West.

ROY LICHTENSTEIN (American, 1923–97)

Famous for: Pop art paintings that reproduce comic book images using small dots of paint

Fascinating fact: Lichtenstein was a gifted musician—he played piano, clarinet, and jazz flute, and started a high school jazz band.

RICHARD LONG (British, born 1945)

Famous for: Turning his walks into art by leaving traces in the landscape or creating texts and sculptures

Fascinating fact: Long's teacher let him paint and draw during assembly, when the other students had to sing hymns.

MORRIS LOUIS (American, 1912–62)

Famous for: Colorful paintings made by pouring paint down the canvas

Fascinating fact: Louis was very secretive about his work—not even his wife was allowed into his studio.

ANNA MARIA MAIOLINO (Brazilian, born Italy 1942)

Famous for: Sculptures made from unfired clay, and drawings in which she cuts, tears, and stitches together paper

Fascinating fact: Maiolino is the youngest of ten brothers and sisters.

PIERO MANZONI (Italian, 1933–63)

Famous for: Creating ninety sealed tin cans filled with his own poop

Fascinating fact: For one of his exhibitions, Manzoni made some hard-boiled eggs, "signed" them with his thumbprint, and then gave them away for the audience to eat.

AGNES MARTIN (American, born Canada, 1912–2004)

Famous for: Subtle abstract paintings featuring grids and lines

Fascinating fact: Martin lived alone her entire adult life and avoided all modern means of communication. Her home had no television, radio, music, or telephone.

ROBERT MORRIS (American, born 1931)

Famous for: Gray plywood structures and sculptures made from felt

Fascinating fact: Morris has choreographed several pieces of contemporary dance and was married to a dancer and choreographer.

ANTONI MUNTADAS (Spanish, born 1942)

Famous for: Multimedia works and public art installations that focus on social and political issues

Fascinating fact: Whenever Muntadas starts a new art project he goes to his favorite place to be inspired: the picture collection of the New York Public Library.

BRUCE NAUMAN (American, born 1941)

Famous for: Performances, videos, installations, and neon sculptures, especially his spiral neon which reads: "The true artist helps the world by revealing mystic truths"

Fascinating fact: Nauman lives and works on a ranch in New Mexico, where he raises horses and cattle.

BARNETT NEWMAN (American, 1905–70)

Famous for: Large paintings featuring lines of color that he called "zips"

Fascinating fact: Newman once ran for election as the mayor of New York City.

CHRIS OFILI (British, born 1968)

Famous for: Using elephant dung in his art

Fascinating fact: Ofili once owned a lime-green car with a horn that made a bellowing sound like an elephant.

CLAES OLDENBURG (American, born Sweden 1929)

Famous for: Giant sculptures of everyday objects such as lipsticks, apple cores, and clothespins

Fascinating fact: Oldenburg moved from Sweden to America when he was six years old. He couldn't speak English, so he and his younger brother created a made-up world complete with detailed maps, newspapers, advertisements, and movie posters.

GABRIEL OROZCO (Mexican, born 1962)

Famous for: Inventive sculptures, including a black-and-white-patterned human skull and a Citroën car with its middle section cut out

Fascinating fact: Orozco is a constant traveler and divides his time between Paris, New York, and Mexico City. He uses his airline tickets and foreign bank notes in many of his artworks.

NAM JUNE PAIK (Korean-American, 1932–2006)

Famous for: Large-scale television-screen and video installations

Fascinating fact: Paik studied music at the University of Tokyo.

BLINKY PALERMO (German, 1943–77)

Famous for: Colorful paintings, often made using strips of fabric

Fascinating fact: Palermo's real name was Peter Schwarze. He was nicknamed Blinky Palermo because he looked like the mafia gangster of the same name.

MICHELANGELO PISTOLETTO (Italian, born 1933)

Famous for: Paintings made directly onto the surfaces of mirrors

Fascinating fact: When he was fourteen years old, Pistoletto began an apprenticeship in his father's art restoration business in Turin, Italy.

JACKSON POLLOCK (American, 1912–56)

Famous for: Paintings made by dripping, throwing, and splashing paint onto the canvas

Fascinating fact: Pollock's life and work were turned into a Hollywood movie starring the actor Ed Harris as the painter.

★

GERHARD RICHTER (German, born 1932)

Famous for: Paintings made in a variety of styles, including multicolored grids and blurry paintings based on photographs

Fascinating fact: At the age of sixteen, Richter left school and trained as an apprentice set-painter in a theater.

★

BRIDGET RILEY (British, born 1931)

Famous for: Op art paintings in which abstract shapes and patterns seem to move and have depth

Fascinating fact: Riley once took shelter in the doorway of a London art gallery to avoid a rainstorm. The owner, Victor Musgrave, invited her in and looked at her artworks—the following year, his gallery presented her first solo exhibition.

★

JUDITH JOY ROSS (American, born 1946)

Famous for: Small black-and-white portrait photographs

Fascinating fact: Ross once received a phone call notifying her that she had won a $25,000 award for her work. She had never heard of the prize, but she gratefully accepted the money.

★

DIETER ROTH (German-Swiss, 1930–88)

Famous for: Artworks made from rotting food including cheese, chocolate, yogurt, and bananas

Fascinating fact: Roth once collaborated with the artist Richard Hamilton on an exhibition for dogs, where all the pictures were hung at dog-eye level.

★

ED RUSCHA (American, born 1937)

Famous for: Paintings of gasoline stations and mountains, which often incorporate words and phrases

Fascinating fact: Ruscha has made art from a wide range of materials, including bolognese sauce, baked beans, daffodils, and grass stains.

★

ROBERT RYMAN (American, born 1930)

Famous for: White paintings on square canvases

Fascinating fact: Ryman came to New York as a young man to pursue a career in jazz. While in the city, he got a job as a security guard at The Museum of Modern Art.

★

NIKI DE SAINT PHALLE (French, 1930–2002)

Famous for: Paintings in which she shot at the canvas with a gun or rifle, and brightly colored, larger-than-life sculptures of women

Fascinating fact: During her twenties, Saint Phalle modeled for *Vogue*, *Life*, and other magazines.

GEORGE SEGAL (American, 1924–2000)

Famous for: Life-size sculptures of people made from unpainted plaster

Fascinating fact: Segal grew up on a poultry farm in New Jersey. After he got married, he bought his own chicken farm where he held annual picnics for his friends from the New York art world.

★

RICHARD SERRA (American, born 1939)

Famous for: Giant public sculptures made from rolled steel

Fascinating fact: One of Serra's most treasured memories is of his fourth birthday, when he was taken to watch the launch of a vast new tanker at the shipyard where his father worked.

★

DO HO SUH (Korean, born 1962)

Famous for: Delicate fabric sculptures of houses including his childhood home in Seoul, Korea, and his apartment in New York

Fascinating fact: Suh has always had a passion for studying fish and wanted to be a marine biologist before he became an artist.

★

ATSUKO TANAKA (Japanese, 1932–2005)

Famous for: Creating an electric dress made from two hundred light bulbs painted red, blue, green, and yellow

Fascinating fact: Tanaka had four older sisters and four older brothers.

★

CY TWOMBLY (American, 1928–2011)

Famous for: Large-scale paintings featuring writing, scrawls, and graffiti

Fascinating fact: Twombly once worked in the army as a cryptographer, deciphering secret codes.

★

ANDY WARHOL (American, 1928–87)

Famous for: Paintings and prints of celebrities and soup cans

Fascinating fact: Warhol had a studio in New York called "The Factory" which became a famous meeting place for artists and socialites, musicians and performers.

★

GILLIAN WEARING (British, born 1963)

Famous for: A series of photographs in which people held up handwritten signs revealing their private thoughts

Fascinating fact: Wearing loves roller coasters and took her partner, the artist Michael Landy, to a theme park on their first date.

★

RACHEL WHITEREAD (British, born 1963)

Famous for: Sculptures cast from household objects and unusual spaces; known especially for casting the inside of an entire house using concrete

Fascinating fact: Whiteread loves to go beachcombing with her two sons on the banks of the Thames River in London, where they have collected old pipes, lead balls, ammunition, and bones.

GLOSSARY

Abstract art
Art based on color and shapes, often geometrical ones. Abstract art does not show clearly recognizable people, places, or objects.

Abstract Expressionism
A style developed by American painters in the 1940s and 1950s. Their art was abstract, and they expressed their thoughts and feelings through colors and shapes rather than by painting people or things.

Art world
The art world is made up of all the people who make, buy, sell, write about, and exhibit works of art.

Assemblage
An artwork in which the artist has gathered together or assembled a collection of everyday objects. It might be a two-dimensional collage or a three-dimensional sculpture.

Autobiography
An autobiography tells the story of someone's own life in a book, play, film, or artwork.

Casting
Pouring liquid material, such as plaster or molten bronze, into a mold. When the liquid sets solid, it is removed to make an artwork.

Collage
Art made by sticking pieces of paper, photographs, newspaper, or fabric onto a surface. Contemporary artists also use computers to create digital collages by cutting and pasting images together.

Conceptual art
Art in which concepts or ideas are just as important as the materials used or the final look of the artwork. Conceptual artists ask questions about what art is, and they often produce performances, photographs, or installations rather than traditional paintings or sculptures.

Found objects
Natural or man-made objects found by an artist and used to inspire or create their artworks.

Graphic design
The art of combining text and images to deliver a message, for example on websites, or in magazines, books, and advertisements.

Installation
The act of hanging, placing, or installing works of art. "Installation" can also be used as a shorthand for "installation art."

Installation art
An artwork usually designed for one particular place and sometimes just for a short period of time. Installation art is often made of many separate parts, and can take up an entire room or gallery.

Interactive artwork
A work of art in which you, the viewer, are encouraged to participate. An interactive artwork is only really made complete when you become involved.

Materials
The physical things needed to make a work of art, such as canvas, plaster, marble, or paint.

Medium / media
A medium is the material or substance an artist uses to make their work, such as paint or video. Media is the plural of medium.

Minimalism / Minimal art
A type of pared-back abstract art that first appeared in the 1960s. Minimal art uses simple, geometric shapes such as squares and rectangles, and is often created from modern industrial materials.

Multimedia artist
An artist who likes to make artworks from many different media or materials, rather than only working in one medium such as painting or sculpture.

Multiple
An artwork made in a number of identical copies by the artist him- or herself. The number produced is usually limited and the copies together are known as an edition.

Op art
An art style developed in the 1960s that created optical effects in painting. Op artists use shapes, lines, and patterns to produce the effect of vibration or depth in their artworks.

Painting
The art of applying paint to a surface to create a picture. A painting usually features paint on canvas, but in contemporary art it can be any artwork that uses paint as the main material, applied to any surface.

Performance art
Art that involves a series of actions usually performed by the artist. The performance can be spontaneous or carefully planned, carried out in private or seen by many people in a public place. This type of art is often documented in photographs, films, and videos.

Photography
The art of taking and printing photographs. Photographs can be black-and-white or color, and can be produced using a film camera or a digital camera.

Pop art
An art that draws its imagery, style, and inspiration from popular culture and mass media, including advertisements, comic strips, and consumer goods.

Primary colors
The three primary colors are red, yellow, and blue. They are "primary" because they can be mixed together in different amounts to create every other color.

Print
An image created by pressing ink onto a sheet of paper or any other surface. The ink can be transferred from a metal plate, a stone, a block of wood, a fabric screen, or a smooth material called linoleum. Photographic prints are made using light-sensitive materials.

Screenprint
A kind of print made using a fabric screen that is stretched tightly over a frame. Areas of the screen that are not going to be printed are blocked out by a stencil. A roller or squeegee is then used to push the ink through the open parts of the fabric onto a sheet of paper.

Sculpture
A three-dimensional artwork usually made by chiseling, modeling, or carving a material such as bronze or wood. Sculptures can also include everyday or found objects.

Self-portrait
A portrait of the artist by the artist. Self-portraits can be drawn, painted, sculpted, or photographed.

Series
A number of artworks by an artist that together form a group. Works in a series will usually be made in the same materials as each other, or share similar imagery.

Studio assistant
Someone who assists in a studio, the place where an artist works. An assistant can help to prepare materials, produce artworks, organize exhibitions, or carry out duties such as paying bills or ordering supplies.

Surrealism / Surrealist art
A style of art that began in the 1920s in which familiar objects are presented in an unexpected or surprising way. The Surrealists were particularly interested in dreams and the unconscious mind.

Three-dimensional
A three-dimensional artwork is one that projects out into space, or has depth, such as a sculpture. The three dimensions refer to the length, width, and depth of the object.

Two-dimensional
A two-dimensional artwork is one made using a flat surface, for instance a painting or photograph. The two dimensions refer to the length and width of the artwork.

Urban intervention
An artwork, performance, or installation in a city that uses parts of the urban environment such as walls, statues, buildings, or parks. Many urban interventions are inspired by the artist's political or environmental concerns.

Video art
Art made using video or television. Video art can take many forms, including recordings shown in a gallery, installations that include television monitors, or live broadcast events.

WHERE TO FIND OUT MORE

The Museum of Modern Art, New York
www.moma.org
Guggenheim Museum, New York
www.guggenheim.org
Dia Art Foundation, New York
www.diacenter.org
Tate, London
www.tate.org.uk
Oxford Art Online
www.oxfordartonline.com
The Art Story
www.theartstory.org
Artcyclopedia
www.artcyclopedia.com

WHERE TO SEE MORE

All of the artworks featured in this book are in the collection of The Museum of Modern Art, New York. Below is a selection of some other great museums with permanent collections of international contemporary art:

NORTH AMERICA
Art Gallery of Ontario, Toronto, Canada
Art Institute of Chicago, Illinois
Dia Art Foundation, New York
Menil Collection, Houston, Texas
Museum of Contemporary Art, Los Angeles, California
National Gallery of Art, Washington
National Gallery of Canada, Ottawa, Canada
Philadelphia Museum of Art, Pennsylvania
San Francisco Museum of Modern Art, California
Solomon R. Guggenheim Museum, New York
Walker Art Center, Minneapolis, Minnesota
Whitney Museum of American Art, New York

EUROPE
Arken Museum of Modern Art, Copenhagen, Denmark
Centre Georges Pompidou, Paris, France
Fondation Beyeler, Basel, Switzerland
Irish Museum of Modern Art, Dublin, Ireland
Kunsthalle Hamburg, Germany
Kunstmuseum Basel, Switzerland
Kunstmuseum Liechtenstein, Vaduz, Liechtenstein
Louisiana Museum of Modern Art, Humlebaek, Denmark
Moderna Museet, Stockholm, Sweden
Moscow Museum of Modern Art, Russia
Musée d'Art Moderne de la Ville de Paris, France
Museo Nacional Centro de Arte Reina Sofía, Madrid, Spain
Museu d'Arte Contemporani de Barcelona, Spain
Pinakothek der Moderne, Munich, Germany
Scottish National Gallery of Modern Art, Edinburgh, Scotland
Staatliche Museen zu Berlin - Neue National Galerie and Hamburger Bahnhof, Museum für Gegenwart, Berlin, Germany
Staatsgalerie Stuttgart, Germany
Stedelijk Museum, Amsterdam, The Netherlands
Stedelijk Museum voor Actuele Kunst (SMAK), Ghent, Belgium
Tate, London, Liverpool and St Ives, UK

REST OF THE WORLD
Gallery of Modern Art, Queensland, Australia
Museum of Contemporary Art, São Paulo University, Brazil
Museum of Contemporary Art, Sydney, Australia
São Paulo Museum of Art, Brazil
Tehran Museum of Contemporary Art, Iran
Tel Aviv Museum of Art, Israel
The National Museum of Modern Art, Tokyo, Japan

PICTURE CREDITS

All works are from the collection of The Museum of Modern Art, New York. Dimensions are given in inches (and feet, where specified), height before width before depth.

p. 1 Atsuko Tanaka, *Untitled*, 1964
Synthetic polymer paint on canvas, 10' 11 1/4" x 7' 4 3/4"
John G. Powers Fund. Photo John Wronn. © 2012 Ryoji Ito

pp. 2–3 Francis Alÿs, *Untitled*, 1994
Oil on canvas and synthetic polymer paint on sheet metal, three panels, small panel by Francis Alÿs 12 1/2" x 10", medium panel by Emilio Rivera 36" x 28 1/8", large panel by Juan Garcia 47 1/4" x 36"
Gift of Eileen and Peter Norton. Courtesy David Zwirner, New York

p. 4 John Chamberlain, *Essex*, 1960
Automobile parts and other metal, 9' x 6' 8" x 43"
Gift of Mr and Mrs Robert C. Scull and purchase. Photo John Wronn. © ARS, NY and DACS, London 2012

p. 5 Damien Hirst, *Round* from *In a Spin, the Action of the World on Things*, Volume 1, 2002
One from a portfolio of twenty-three etching, aquatint, and drypoints, sheet 35 7/8" x 27 1/2"
The Associates Fund. Photo Thomas Griesel. © Hirst Holdings Limited and Damien Hirst. All rights reserved, DACS 2012

p. 8 Yves Klein, *Anthropometry: Princess Helena*, 1961
Oil on paper on wood, 6' 6" x 50 1/2"
Gift of Mr and Mrs Arthur Wiesenberger. Photo Mali Olatunji. © ADAGP, Paris and DACS, London 2012

p. 9 Olafur Eliasson, *The colour spectrum series*, 2005
Series of forty-eight photogravures, composition (each) 10 9/16" x 18 1/8"; sheet (each) 13 9/16" x 17 15/16". Publisher Niels Borch Jensen Verlag and Galerie, Berlin. Printer Niels Borch Jensen Værksted for Koppertryk, Copenhagen. Edition 18
Riva Castleman Endowment Fund. Photo John Wronn. © Olafur Eliasson

p. 10 Dan Flavin, *"monument" 1 for V. Tatlin*, 1964
Fluorescent lights and metal fixtures, 8' x 23 1/8" x 4 1/2"
Gift of UBS. © ARS, NY and DACS, London 2012

p. 11 Bruce Nauman, *Human/Need/Desire*, 1983
Neon tubing and wire with glass tubing suspension frames, 7' 10 3/8" x 70 1/2" x 25 3/4"
Gift of Emily and Jerry Spiegel. © ARS, NY and DACS, London 2012

p. 12 Jackson Pollock, *White Light*, 1954
Oil, enamel, and aluminum paint on canvas, 48 1/4" x 38 1/4"
The Sidney and Harriet Janis Collection. Photo Paige Knight. © The Pollock-Krasner Foundation, ARS, NY, and DACS, London 2012

p. 13 left Roy Lichtenstein, *Girl with Ball*, 1961
Oil on canvas, 60 1/4" x 36 1/4"
Gift of Philip Johnson. Photo Kate Keller. © The Estate of Roy Lichtenstein / DACS 2012

p. 13 right Bridget Riley, *Current*, 1964
Synthetic polymer paint on composition board, 58 3/8" x 58 7/8"
Philip Johnson Fund. © Bridget Riley 2012. All rights reserved. Courtesy Karsten Schubert, London

p. 14 Cy Twombly, *Untitled*, 1970
Oil-based house paint and crayon on canvas, 13' 3 3/8" x 21' 1/8"
Acquired through the Lillie P. Bliss Bequest and The Sidney and Harriet Janis Collection (both by exchange). © Cy Twombly

p. 15 left Robert Morris, *Untitled*, 1969
Felt, 15' 3/4" x 6' 1/2" x 1"
The Gilman Foundation Fund. © ARS, NY and DACS, London 2012

p. 15 right Nam June Paik, *Untitled*, 1993
Player piano, fifteen televisions, two cameras, two laser disc players, one electric light and light bulb, and wires, overall approx. 8' 4" x 8' 9" x 48", including laser disc player and lamp
Bernhill Fund, Gerald S. Elliot Fund, gift of Margot Paul Ernst, and purchase. © 2012 Estate of Nam June Paik

p. 16 Gillian Wearing, *Self Portrait at 17 Years Old*, 2003
Framed chromogenic color print, 45 1/2" x 36 1/4"
Acquired through the generosity of The Contemporary Arts Council of The Museum of Modern Art. Photo Thomas Griesel. Courtesy Maureen Paley, London

p. 17 Chuck Close, *Self-Portrait*, 1997
Oil on canvas, 8' 6" x 7'
Gift of Agnes Gund, Jo Carole and Ronald S. Lauder, Donald L. Bryant, Jr, Leon Black, Michael and Judy Ovitz, Anna Marie and Robert F. Shapiro, Leila and Melville Straus, Doris and Donald Fisher, and purchase. Photo Paige Knight. © Chuck Close. Courtesy The Pace Gallery, New York

p. 18 Richard Long, *Kilkenny Circle*, 1984
Stones, 8' 10 1/4" diameter
Gift of the Dannheisser Foundation. Photo Jonathan Muzikar. © Richard Long. All Rights Reserved, DACS 2012

p. 19 left Damien Hirst, *Round* from *In a Spin, the Action of the World on Things*, Volume 1, 2002
One from a portfolio of twenty-three etching, aquatint, and drypoints, sheet 35 7/8" x 27 1/2"
The Associates Fund. Photo Thomas Griesel. © Hirst Holdings Limited and Damien Hirst. All rights reserved, DACS 2012

p. 19 right Atsuko Tanaka, *Untitled*, 1964
Synthetic polymer paint on canvas, 10' 11 1/4" x 7' 4 3/4"
John G. Powers Fund. Photo John Wronn. © 2012 Ryoji Ito

p. 20 Nicolas Lampert, *Very Slow, Very Tired*, 2006
Digital print, composition (irregular) 31" x 55"; sheet 44" x 62 3/4". Publisher Nicolas Lampert, Milwaukee, Wisconsin. Printer Prime Digital Media, New Berlin, Wisconsin. Edition unlimited, in varying scales
Fund for the Twenty-First Century. Photo Thomas Griesel. © Nicolas Lampert 2012

p. 21 Joan Fontcuberta and Pere Formiguera, *Alopex Stultus*, 1985–88
One from a series of gelatin silver prints and ink with watercolor on paper, overall 16 13/16" x 14 7/8"
Lois and Bruce Zenkel Fund. Photo Thomas Griesel. © DACS 2012

p. 22 James Lee Byars, *The Table of Perfect*, 1989
Gold leaf on white marble, 39 1/4" x 39 1/4" x 39 1/4"
Committee on Painting and Sculpture Funds. © The Estate of James Lee Byars

p. 23 left Martín Azúa, *Basic House*, 1999
Polyester, 6' 6 3/4" x 6' 6 3/4" x 6' 6 3/4"
Gift of Martín Azúa. Photo Daniel Riera

p. 23 right Agnes Martin, *Friendship*, 1963
Incised gold leaf and gesso on canvas, 6' 3" x 6' 3"
Fractional and promised gift of Celeste and Armand P. Bartos. © 2012 Agnes Martin / DACS

p. 24 Morris Louis, *Beta Lambda*, 1961
Synthetic polymer paint on canvas, 8' 7 3/8" x 13' 4 1/4"
Gift of Mrs Abner Brenner. © 1961 Morris Louis

p. 25 left Daniel Buren, *White Acrylic Painting on White and Anthracite Gray Striped Fabric*, 1966
Synthetic polymer paint on striped cotton fabric, 7' 5 3/4" x 6' 5 5/8"
Nina and Gordon Bunshaft Bequest and the Philip L. Goodwin Collection Funds (both by exchange). Photo John Wronn. © ADAGP, Paris and DACS, London 2012

p. 25 right Eduardo Chillida, *Untitled*, 1966
Ink on paper, 39 3/8" x 27 5/8"
The Joan and Lester Avnet Collection. Photo Jonathan Muzikar. © Zabalaga-Leku, DACS, London 2012

p. 26 Joseph Beuys, *Felt Suit*, 1970
Multiple of felt, overall 69 7/8" x 28 1/8" x 5 5/16" (irregular). Publisher Galerie René Block, Berlin. Fabricator unknown. Edition 100
The Associates Fund. © DACS 2012

p. 27 Vito Acconci, *Adjustable Wall Bra*, 1990–91
Plaster, steel, canvas, light, lightbulbs, and audio equipment, overall installation dimensions variable, 13' 9" x 17' 4" x 13' 6"
Sid R. Bass Fund and purchase. Courtesy Acconci Studio

p. 28 Claes Oldenburg, *Two Cheeseburgers, with Everything (Dual Hamburgers)*, 1962
Burlap soaked in plaster, painted with enamel, 7" x 14 3/4" x 8 5/8"
Philip Johnson Fund. Courtesy the Oldenburg van Bruggen Studio. © 1962 Claes Oldenburg

p. 29 above Felix Gonzalez-Torres, *"Untitled" (Perfect Lovers)*, 1991
Clocks, paint on wall, overall 14" x 28" x 2 3/4"
Gift of the Dannheisser Foundation. © The Felix Gonzalez-Torres Foundation. Courtesy Andrea Rosen Gallery, New York

p. 29 below Judith Joy Ross, *The Stewart Sisters, H.F. Grebey Junior High School, Hazleton, Pennsylvania*, 1992
Gelatin silver printing-out-paper print, 9 3/4" x 7 11/16"
Gift of Patricia Lawrence. © Judith Joy Ross. Courtesy Pace/MacGill Gallery, New York

p. 30 Marcel Broodthaers, *White Cabinet and White Table*, 1965
Painted cabinet, table, and eggshells, cabinet 33 7/8" x 32 1/4" x 24 1/2", table 41" x 39 3/8" x 15 3/4"
Fractional and promised gift of Jo Carole and Ronald S. Lauder. © DACS 2012

p. 31 left Robert Ryman, *Classico 5*, 1968
Synthetic polymer paint on paper, overall 93 1/4" x 88 1/2"
Purchased with funds provided by the Committee on Drawings, Richard S. Zeisler Bequest (by exchange), the estate of William S. Lieberman, The Edward John Noble Foundation, Kathy and Richard S. Fuld Jr, Marie-Josée and Henry R. Kravis, Marlene Hess and Jim Zirin, The Judith Rothschild Foundation, Sally and Wynn Kramarsky, Sharon Percy Rockefeller, and Aaron Fleischman. Photo John Wronn. © 2012 Robert Ryman / DACS, London

p. 31 right Piero Manzoni, *Achrome*, 1962
Fiberglass on velvet-covered wood, 32" x 25 1/2" x 10 3/8"
Nina and Gordon Bunshaft Bequest, Mrs. John Hay Whitney Bequest, and Donald B. Marron Funds. © DACS 2012

p. 32 Andreas Gursky, *Bahrain I*, 2005
Chromogenic color print, 9' 10 7/8" x 7' 2 1/2"
Acquired in honor of Robert B. Menschel through the generosity of Agnes Gund, Marie-Josée and Henry R. Kravis, Ronald S. and Jo Carole Lauder, and the Speyer Family Foundation. Photo Jonathan Muzikar. Courtesy Gallery Sprueth/Magers © DACS, London 2012

p. 33 Gerhard Richter, *Flugzeug II (Airplane II)*, 1966
Screenprint, composition 19 1/8" x 32 1/16"; sheet 24" x 33 7/8". Publisher Galerie Rottloff, Karlsruhe, Germany. Printer: Löw Siebdruck, Stuttgart, Germany. Edition 20
Ann and Lee Fensterstock Fund, Alexandra Herzan Fund, and Virginia Cowles Schroth Fund. Photo David Allison. © Gerhard Richter 2012

p. 34 Niki de Saint Phalle, *Shooting Painting American Embassy*, 1961
Paint, plaster, wood, plastic bags, shoe, twine, metal seat, axe, metal can, toy gun, wire mesh, bullet, and other objects on wood, 8' 3/8" x 25 7/8" x 8 5/8"
Gift of the Niki Charitable Art Foundation. Photo John Wronn. © ADAGP, Paris and DACS, London 2012

p. 35 Lucio Fontana, *Spatial Concept: Expectations*, 1960
Slashed canvas and gauze, 39 1/2" x 31 5/8"
Gift of Philip Johnson. Photo Thomas Griesel. © Lucio Fontana / SIAE / DACS, London 2012

p. 36 Martin Kippenberger, *Martin, Into the Corner, You Should Be Ashamed of Yourself*, 1992
Cast aluminum, clothing, and iron plate, 71 1/2" x 29 1/2" x 13 1/2"
Blanchette Hooker Rockefeller Fund Bequest, Anna Marie and Robert F. Shapiro, Jerry I. Speyer, and Michael and Judy Ovitz Funds. © Estate Martin Kippenberger, Galerie Gisela Capitain, Cologne

p. 37 left George Segal, *The Bus Driver*, 1962
Plaster over cheesecloth; bus parts including coin box, steering wheel, driver's seat, railing, and dashboard, over wood and cinder blocks, overall 7' 5" x 51 5/8" x 6' 4 3/4"
Philip Johnson Fund. © The George and Helen Segal Foundation / DACS, London / VAGA, New York 2012

p. 37 right Michelangelo Pistoletto, *Man with Yellow Pants*, 1964
Paper, oil, and pencil on polished stainless steel, 6' 6 7/8" x 39 3/8"
Blanchette Hooker Rockefeller Fund. Photo Thomas Griesel. © Fondazione Pistoletto-Cittadellarte, Biella

p. 38 Chris Ofili, *Prince Amongst Thieves*, 1999
Synthetic polymer paint, oil, paper collage, polyester glitter, resin, map pins, and elephant dung on canvas, 8' x 6'
Mimi and Peter Haas Fund. © Chris Ofili. Courtesy Victoria Miro Gallery, London. Photo Stephen White

p. 39 left Dieter Roth, *Basel on the Rhine*, 1969
Chocolate and steel, 31 1/2" x 31 1/2" x 1 3/4"
Barbara Jakobson Fund and Jeanne C. Thayer Fund. © Dieter Roth Estate. Courtesy Hauser & Wirth

p. 39 right John Chamberlain, *Essex*, 1960
Automobile parts and other metal, 9' x 6' 8" x 43"
Gift of Mr and Mrs Robert C. Scull and purchase. Photo John Wronn. © ARS, NY and DACS, London 2012

p. 40 Francis Alÿs, *Untitled*, 1994
Oil on canvas and synthetic polymer paint on sheet metal, three panels, small panel by Francis Alÿs 12 1/2" x 10", medium panel by Emilio Rivera 36" x 28 1/8", large panel by Juan Garcia 47 1/4" x 36"
Gift of Eileen and Peter Norton. Courtesy David Zwirner, New York

p. 41 Vija Celmins, *To Fix the Image in Memory*, 1977–82
Stones and painted bronze, eleven pairs, dimensions variable
Gift of Edward R. Broida in honor of David and Renee McKee. Photo Thomas Griesel. Courtesy McKee Gallery, New York

p. 42 Barnett Newman, *Broken Obelisk*, 1963–69
Cor-Ten steel, 24' 7 1/4" x 10' 5 1/2" x 10' 5 1/2"
Given anonymously. Photo David Allison. © ARS, NY and DACS, London 2012

p. 43 above Peter Fischli and David Weiss, *The Way Things Go*, 1987
16mm film transferred to video, 31 minutes
Purchase. © Peter Fischli, David Weiss. Courtesy Matthew Marks Gallery, New York

p. 43 below Richard Serra, *One Ton Prop (House of Cards)*, 1969 (refabricated 1986)
Lead antimony, four plates, each 48" x 48" x 1"
Gift of the Grinstein Family. © ARS, NY and DACS, London 2012

p. 44 Do Ho Suh, *Doormat: Welcome*, 1998
Multiple of polyurethane rubber, 18 7/8" x 28 1/8" x 1 1/4". Edition 5
Robert and Anna Marie Shapiro Fund. Photo Peter Butler. © Do Ho Suh, 1998. Courtesy the artist and Lehmann Maupin Gallery, New York

p. 45 above Ed Ruscha, *OOF*, 1962 (reworked 1963)
Oil on canvas, 71 1/2" x 67"
Gift of Agnes Gund, the Louis and Bessie Adler Foundation, Inc., Robert and Meryl Meltzer, Jerry I. Speyer, Anna Marie and Robert F. Shapiro, Emily and Jerry Spiegel, an anonymous donor, and purchase. Photo Thomas Griesel. © Ed Ruscha

p. 45 below Antoni Muntadas, *On Translation: Warning*, 1999–present
From a portfolio of twelve examples of ephemeral print projects including one newspaper, one poster, four stickers, and six exhibition announcements, composition and sheet (each): various dimensions. Various publishers. Various editions
The Associates Fund. © Muntadas

p. 46 Chris Burden, *Medusa's Head*, 1990
Plywood, steel, cement, rock, model railroad trains and tracks, 14' diameter
Gift of Sid and Mercedes Bass. © Chris Burden. Courtesy Gagosian Gallery

p. 47 left Anna Maria Maiolino, *Buraco Preto (Black Hole)* from the series "Os Buracos/Desenhos Objetos" (Holes/Drawing Objects), 1974
Torn paper, 27" x 27"
Purchase. © Anna Maria Maiolino

p. 47 right Lee Bontecou, *Untitled*, 1961
Welded steel, canvas, black fabric, rawhide, copper wire, and soot, 6' 8 1/4" x 7' 5" x 34 3/4"
Kay Sage Tanguy Fund. Photo Jonathan Muzikar. © 2012 Lee Bontecou

p. 48 Donald Judd, *Untitled (Stack)*, 1967
Lacquer on galvanized iron, twelve units, each 9" x 40" x 31", installed vertically with 9" intervals
Helen Acheson Bequest (by exchange) and gift of Joseph Helman. © Judd Foundation. Licensed by VAGA, New York / DACS, London 2012

p. 49 Andy Warhol, *Campbell's Soup Cans*, 1962
Synthetic polymer paint on thirty-two canvases, each canvas 20" x 16"
Partial gift of Irving Blum. © The Andy Warhol Foundation for the Visual Arts / ARS, New York / DACS, London 2012

p. 50 John Coplans, *Self Portrait*, 1985
Gelatin silver print, 13 1/8" x 16 7/8"
Gift of Peter MacGill. © The John Coplans Trust

p. 51 Janine Antoni, *Butterfly Kisses*, 1996–99
Cover Girl Thick Lash Mascara on paper, 29 3/4" x 30"
Purchase. Photo John Wronn. Courtesy the artist and Luhring Augustine, New York

p. 52 Jeff Koons, *Three Ball 50/50 Tank (Two Dr. J. Silver Series, One Wilson Supershot)*, 1985
Glass, painted steel, distilled water, plastic, and three basketballs, 60 5/8" x 48 3/4" x 13 1/4"
Gift of Werner and Elaine Dannheisser. Photo John Wronn. © Jeff Koons

p. 53 above Blinky Palermo, *Flipper*, 1970
Screenprint on two sheets, composition (each approx.) 31 1/2" x 23 5/8"; sheet (each) 33 3/4" x 25 15/16". Publisher Galerie Heiner Friedrich, Munich / New York. Printer Atelier Laube, Munich. Edition 90
Walter Bareiss Fund and Sarah C. Epstein Fund. © DACS 2012

p. 53 below Gabriel Orozco, *Horses Running Endlessly*, 1995
Wood, 3 3/8" x 34 3/8" x 34 3/8"
Gift of Agnes Gund and Lewis B. Cullman in honor of Chess in the Schools. © Gabriel Orozco. Courtesy Marian Goodman Gallery, New York

p. 54 Rachel Whiteread, *Untitled (Mattress)*, 1991
Plaster, 12" x 6' 2" x 54"
Gift of Agnes Gund. Photo Thomas Griesel. © Rachel Whiteread

p. 55 Louise Bourgeois, *Bed #1, state I*, 1997
Etching, drypoint and engraving with watercolor, ink and pencil additions, plate 16 3/8" x 19 3/4", sheet 20 1/16" x 22 13/16". Unpublished state. Printer Harlan & Weaver, New York. Early state before the edition of 100
Gift of the artist. © Louise Bourgeois Trust / DACS, London / VAGA, New York 2012

INDEX

Page numbers in **bold** refer to illustrations

A

Abstract Expressionist 13
Acconci, Vito 27, **27**
Alÿs, Francis **2–3**, 40, **40**
Antoni, Janine 51, **51**
assemblage 34
Azúa, Martín 23, **23**

B

Beuys, Joseph 26, **26**
Bontecou, Lee 47, **47**
Bourgeois, Louise 55, **55**
Broodthaers, Marcel 30, **30**
Burden, Chris **46**, 47
Buren, Daniel 25, **25**
Byars, James Lee 22, **22**

C

Cage, John 15
Celmins, Vija 41, **41**
Chamberlain, John **4**, 39, **39**
Chillida, Eduardo 25, **25**
Close, Chuck 17, **17**
collages 20
color 7, 8–9, 10, 13, 19, 24, 30, 31, 33, 53
- black 25, 33, 47, 50, 53
- blue 8, 9, 10, 53
- gold, 22–23
- gray 14, 25
- green 9, 10, 33, 48
- orange 9
- pink 10, 33
- red 9, 10, 53
- silver 23
- ultraviolet 10
- violet 9
- white 10, 14, 25, 30–31, 53
- yellow 10

conceptual artist 40
Coplans, John 50, **50**

D

drawing 6, 25, 49, 51

E

Eliasson, Olafur 9, **9**

F

film 26, 43
Fischli, Peter and Weiss, David 43, **43**
Flavin, Dan 10, **10**
Fontana, Lucio 35, **35**
Fontcuberta, Joan 21, **21**
Formiguera, Pere 21, **21**

G

Gonzales-Torres, Felix 29, **29**
Gursky, Andreas **32**, 33

H

Hirst, Damien **5**, 19, **19**

I

installation 6, 27, 40, 45, 48

J

Judd, Donald 48, **48**

K

Kippenberger, Martin 36, **36**
Klein, Yves 8, **8**
Koons, Jeff 52, **52**

L

Lampert, Nicolas 20, **20**
Lichtenstein, Roy 13, **13**
Long, Richard 18, **18**, 19
Louis, Morris 24, **24**

M

Maiolino, Anna Maria 47, **47**
Manzoni, Piero 31, **31**
Martin, Agnes 23, **23**
materials 28, 39, 43, 47
- aluminum 36
- asphalt 33
- balloons 43
- bandages 37
- basketballs 52
- bread rolls 31
- bronze 6, 41
- bus seats 37
- cabinets 30
- candles 43
- canvas 13, 14, 24, 27, 31, 35, 47
- cardboard 33
- cars 6, 39
- cement 47
- cheese 39
- chocolate 6, 39

[*materials cont.*]
- clay 31
- clocks 29
- cloth 25, 28
- conveyor belts 47
- cotton padding 31
- crayon 14
- cups 43
- diner counter 37
- eggs/eggshells 7, 30, 39
- elephant dung 6, 39
- fat 26
- felt 15, 26
- fiberglass wool 31
- footprints 18
- furniture 30
- fuse wire 43
- glitter 39
- gold 22–23
- gold leaf 22, 23
- granite 25
- ink 6, 19, 33
- iron 25
- jeans 36
- ladders 43
- lead 43
- light 7, 10–11, 27
- lightbulbs 10, 19, 39
- magazine cutouts 39
- map pins 39
- marble 6, 22
- mascara 51
- masking tape 31
- mattresses 43
- metal plates 43
- metal seats 34
- mirrors 37
- model railroad trains 39, 47
- neon 11
- oil drums 43
- paint 6, 8, 13, 14, 31, 34, 51
- paper 8, 19, 25, 31, 47, 51
- park benches 37
- pianos 15
- pine needles 18
- plaster 28, 37, 54
- rabbit skin 31
- ramps 43
- rawhide 47
- resin 54
- rocks 47
- rubber 44, 54
- scrap metal 39
- seesaws 43

[*materials cont.*]
- shirts 36
- shoes 34, 36
- slate 18
- soot 47
- steel 15, 25, 28, 39, 42, 47
- stickers 45
- stones 18, 41
- street signs 37
- suits 26
- tables 30
- television screens 15
- tires 43
- toy guns 34
- watercolors 49
- wood 18, 25

Minimalist artist 48
Morris, Robert 15, **15**
multimedia artist 45
Muntadas, Antoni 45, **45**

N

Nauman, Bruce 11, **11**
Newman, Barnett 42, **42**

O

Ofili, Chris **38**, 39
Oldenburg, Claes 28, **28**
Op art 13
Orozco, Gabriel 53, **53**

P

Paik, Nam June 15, **15**
painting 6, 13, 14, 17, 19, 23, 24, 25, 30, 34, 35, 37, 39, 40, 45, 48, 49
Palermo, Blinky 53, **53**
pattern 33, 41, 53
performance 6, 8, 34, 51
photography 6, 17, 18, 20, 21, 26, 29, 33, 45, 50
Pistoletto, Michelangelo 37, **37**
Pollock, Jackson **12**, 13
Pop artist 28
print 9, 19, 33, 49, 53, 55

R

Richter, Gerhard 33, **33**
Riley, Bridget 13, **13**
Ross, Judith Joy 29, **29**
Roth, Dieter 39, **39**
Ruscha, Ed 45, **45**
Ryman, Robert 31, **31**

S

Saint Phalle, Niki de 34, **34**
screenprint 33
sculpture 6, 10, 15, 18, 19, 25, 28, 30, 35, 36, 37, 39, 42, 43, 47, 48, 54
Segal, George 37, **37**
Serra, Richard 43, **43**
shape 7, 8, 10, 11, 15, 18, 33, 48
- boxes 48
- circles 17, 18–19, 47
- crosses 18
- cubes 22, 48
- grids 23, 31
- lines 7, 13, 18, 19, 23, 24–25, 31
- ovals 17
- rectangles 31, 48
- spirals 18
- stripes 25
- triangles 17

studio 19, 24
studio assistant 14
Suh, Do Ho 44, **44**
Surrealist art 30

T

Tanaka, Atsuko **1**, 19, **19**
techniques/tools
- blades 35
- brushes 13, 25
- cast/casting 36, 41, 54
- eyelashes 51
- fabric screen 33
- knives 13
- "living paintbrushes" 8
- needles 19
- rollers 8
- screwdrivers 19
- sponges 8
- stencils 33
- trowels 13

Twombly, Cy 14, **14**

U

urban interventions 45

V

video art 6, 15, 45

W

Warhol, Andy 49, **49**
Wearing, Gillian **16**, 17
Whiteread, Rachel 54, **54**

For Clara, Louis, Joe, Harry,
and the next generation of art lovers

ABOUT THE AUTHORS

Jacky Klein studied at Oxford University and the Courtauld Institute of Art, London. Formerly a curator at London's Hayward Gallery and an assistant curator at Tate Modern, she is the author of *Grayson Perry* (Thames & Hudson, 2009). She works in publishing and lives in London.

Suzy Klein studied at Oxford University and City University, London. She writes and broadcasts on the arts and culture, presenting widely on BBC television and radio, and is a contributor to the *Guardian* newspaper and *New Statesman* magazine. She lives in London with her husband and two children.

ACKNOWLEDGMENTS

Our thanks go to Christopher Hudson, Kara Kirk, and the publications, education, and curatorial departments at The Museum of Modern Art, New York, for their guidance, knowledge, and collaborative spirit throughout; to Jamie Camplin at Thames & Hudson for his original thinking in conceiving this book; to the dedicated and hardworking team at Thames & Hudson who have so beautifully realized this book; to the picture researcher, Jo Walton; to Gilda Williams whose early ideas played a part in the shaping of this project; to Mary Jordan, Head of Art, and the grade four children of Mr. Kish's 2011 art class at the American School, London, for their enthusiasm and thoughtful insights; and to Theo for his razor-sharp editorial skills and endless supply of age-appropriate adjectives. Finally, our enduring love and thanks to Mum, Dad, James, and Granny P for their unstinting encouragement, support, and babysitting.

Front cover: Claes Oldenburg, *Two Cheeseburgers, with Everything (Dual Hamburgers)*, 1962
Burlap soaked in plaster, painted with enamel, 7" x 14 3/4" x 8 5/8". The Museum of Modern Art, New York. Philip Johnson Fund. Courtesy the Oldenburg van Bruggen Studio. © 1962 Claes Oldenburg

Endpapers: Janine Antoni, *Butterfly Kisses*, 1996–99 [detail]
Cover Girl Thick Lash Mascara on paper, 29 3/4" x 30". The Museum of Modern Art, New York. Purchase. Photo John Wronn. Courtesy the artist and Luhring Augustine, New York

The Museum of Modern Art
11 West 53rd Street, New York
New York 10019
www.moma.org

Published by arrangement with Thames & Hudson Ltd, London

Second printing 2016

Library of Congress Control Number: 2012937608

ISBN 978-0-87070-809-1

Printed and bound in China through Asia Pacific Offset Ltd